COLLECTED
POEMS
1958–1970

COLLECTED
POEMS
1958 - 1970

GEORGE MACBETH

MACMILLAN

© George MacBeth 1971

SBN boards: 333 12588 6
SBN paper: 333 12589 4

Published by
MACMILLAN AND CO LTD
London and Basingstoke
Associated companies in New York Toronto
Dublin Melbourne Johannesburg & Madras

Printed in Great Britain by
THE BOWERING PRESS
Plymouth

For you

ACKNOWLEDGEMENTS

The author would like to thank The Scorpion Press for permission to reprint a number of poems from *The Broken Places* and *A Doomsday Book*.

CONTENTS

FOREWORD

The poems in the five sections of this book are drawn from about ten years' work. Within sections, the grouping is very roughly chronological, but the sections themselves aim to gather together four main kinds of poem. In the first section, the theme is public crisis, interleaved with family deaths. In the second section I have tried to offer my own kind of white goddess poem. Section three groups together poems written for those who (like myself) regard themselves as children. The fourth section includes poems written primarily for performance : thousands have heard them read, and perhaps those who haven't will treat them as scores rather than texts. In the last section, I have included only new poems.

I

EARLY WARNING

Lord god of wings, forgive this hand
That stole from thee. These holy bones
Where thy long shadow ran I give
Thee back, repentant. From thy dead
Steel bird's ripped belly I and four
Doomed ice-men took them out, eight hands

Fouling thy sacred felled limbs. Two
Dropped bones I stooped and kicked. Forgive
Me, god. I never knew thy bones,
Delivered from the ice, could rise
And kill four men. I thought thou wast
Mortal as I. Thy lofty skull,

Smoothed by the Greenland wind, I stole
With my scarred hands. I thought last night
That whale-fat poured in thy round eyes
Would staunch the wind. If my hut stands
And others fell, no other cause
I seek for that. So when at dawn

Four ice-men died, burnt up by thy
Bones' wrath, I thought : this jealous god's
Enduring skull, strong thigh-bone, I
Must give back safe, wise helps, sure harms
For cruel men. Forgive me, god,
For what I did. Those men thou burned

With inward hell that made them twist
In wrangling heaps were faithless. I
Repent my sin. If I should carve
A cross for thee, draped with a fish
Nailed through its hanging tail, wouldst thou
Dismiss this pain ? I feel it come

Below the eyes, inside my head,
As they all said it came. Forgive
My theft. I give thee back thy skull,
Thy scalding thigh-bone, god. Thou shalt
Own all I have, my hut, my wife,
My friendly pack of dogs, if thou

Wilt only tell why these green scars
Ache in my cheeks ; why this grey mould
Forms on my herring pail ; why this
Right hand that touched thy head shrinks up ;
And why this living fish I touched
Writhes on that plank, spoiled food for gulls ?

THE GOD OF LOVE

'The musk-ox is accustomed to near-Arctic conditions.
When danger threatens, these beasts cluster together to
form a defensive wall or a "porcupine" with the calves in
the middle.'

Dr Wolfgang Engelhardt: 'Survival of the Free'.

I found them between far hills, by a frozen lake,
    On a patch of bare ground. They were grouped
In a solid ring, like an ark of horn. And around
    Them circled, slowly closing in,
Their tongues lolling, their ears flattened against the wind,

A whirlpool of wolves. As I breathed, one fragment of
    bone and
    Muscle detached itself from the mass and
Plunged. The pad of the pack slackened, as if
    A brooch had been loosened. But when the bull
Returned to the herd, the revolving collar was tighter. And
    only

The windward owl, uplifted on white wings
    In the glass of air, alert for her young,
Soared high enough to look into the cleared centre
    And grasp the cause. To the slow brain
Of each beast by the frozen lake what lay in the cradle of
    their crowned

Heads of horn was a sort of god-head. Its brows
    Nudged when the ark was formed. Its need
Was a delicate womb away from the iron collar
    Of death, a cave in the ring of horn
Their encircling flesh had backed with fur. That the collar
    of death

Was the bone of their own skulls : that a softer womb
    Would open between far hills in a plunge
Of bunched muscles : and that their immortal calf lay
    Dead on the snow with its horns dug into
The ice for grass : they neither saw nor felt. And yet if

That hill of fur could split and run — like a river
    Of ice in thaw, like a broken grave —
It would crack across the icy crust of withdrawn
    Sustenance and the rigid circle
Of death be shivered : the fed herd would entail its under-
    fur

On the swell of a soft hill and the future be sown
    On grass, I thought. But the herd fell
By the bank of the lake on the plain, and the pack closed,
    And the ice remained. And I saw that the god
In their ark of horn was a god of love, who made them die.

A CONFESSION

Was it alive ? I often asked myself
And avoided the answer. I called it something cooking,
Curled up and rising, soft shapeless matter
Stuck to my greased sides waiting to be born.
But once or twice in the small hours I lay thinking
That it could feel things : it was warm in its wet cave,
Swimming and feeding like a baby shrimp there ;
And then the hard cold inrush of its killer,
Saw-teeth, threshing fins, cascading water,
And the soul spat like a bubble out of its head,
Three months old. I don't know when they're shaped
Like things you can see are children. I was afraid
To look the books up. I've imagined monsters
At three months : or at best like pancake men,
Things from a dream, radiation monsters.
Under the anaesthetic I dreamed nothing.
But one night for the pain they gave me morphia.
I had a strange dream then, worse than a nightmare.
I was in the baby : do you follow me ? *in* it.
I'd felt them pull it out : then it grew huge,
Filled the small ward, it was throbbing bloody matter
Soft inside like a cooling hot-cross bun,
And I was in the middle, six blobs of dough
Not feeling anything. Then I woke up
Sweating with pain : no baby, nothing but darkness
Ticking with clocks, dripping with water, and blood
From clots of cotton-wool sopping through my night-
    dress.
It was me in pain : and I'd thought my baby was
That never lived perhaps to feel a pain.
I felt relaxed, free, till the pain began.
It wasn't bad at first : just aching rubbing
From an internal graze : but it was agony
Like ripping bandages from the middle of my guts

When the plugs came out. It became routine.
Each morning, screens : and forceps picking at me,
Dismembering the corpse in penny numbers.
That last day was the worst. Like having the curse
Worse than when it's worst. I was having a baby
Born in bits. I could recognise it then :
Solid : not blood : I could see cells and things.
For two months since I've kept on wondering
Did it all come out ? They said I'd take
A while to adjust to it, but I know for sure
It might be growing again from one bit left,
A resurrected monster, like a giant lizard
Sprung from a tadpole, gathering itself for revenge
On me and its father. This last half-hour
I've started noticing the Virgin Mary
Above the altar. Suppose she'd not believed
She was to be Christ's mother, taken precautions,
Aborted Him. Would anyone have blamed her
For not being taken in by wishful visions ?
She was, though. She believed what she was told
And the child was born that God was Father to,
Planted by the angel. Listen, now : suppose
I was the victim of an angel, too,
One with powerful fins and the ability to live
Between these pink doors for days without weakening
Or dropping his wand. Only two people would know
If Christ came back I might have murdered Him
And you'd be one of them. You've said on Sundays
We're punished for our sins. What could mine be
For crucifying someone in my womb ?

18

MOTHER SUPERIOR

Sisters, it will be necessary
To prepare a cool retreat. See to
It that several basins are filled
Nightly with fresh water and placed there.
Take care that food for a long stay be

Provided in sealed jars. I know of
No way to protect an outer room
From the light but some must be tried. Let
The walls be made thick to keep out the
Heat. Before the Annunciation

Our Lord exacts no other service.
It may seem prudent to wear a wool
Robe at all times and to bow down when
The Word comes. Remember the parable
Of the Virgins and pray for all the

Unpremeditating. 'The brides of
Our Lord in their burrows' may not be
A flattering title but the known
Future lies in the wombs of prepared
Rabbits. To bear a pure strain with no

Care for the world's corruption requires
Courage, sisters. Creating a safe
Place for the incarnation of what
One can scarcely imagine without
Madness might seem a demeaning task.

In the Order of Resurrection
Of which you are acolytes there is
No more noble service. Remember
The Code. Your duty is not to the
Sick but to the unborn. Perform it.

THE KILLING

In a wooden room, surrounded by lights and
    Faces, the place where death had
Come to its sharpest point was exposed. In a
    Clear shell they examined the
    Needle of death. How many
  Million deaths were concentrated in

A single centre ! The compass of death was
    Lifted, detached and broken,
Taken and burned. The seed of death lay in the
    Hold. Without disturbance or
    Ceremony they sealed it
  In foil. The ship stirred at the quay. The

Pilot was ready. A long shadow slanted
    On the harbour water. The
Fin bearing the ignorant crew on their brief
    Journey cut through the air. Three
    Furlongs out at sea the
  Strike of the engine fell. The screws turned

At ease on the rim of the world. The hour had
    Come. The action was taken.
The doors opened. And the ash went out to sea
    Borne with the moon on the tide
    Away from the shore towards the
  Open water. The shell rocked on the

Livid waves. The captain washed his hands in the
    Salt to cleanse the illusion
Of blood. The light casket lay on the soaked planks
    Emptied of all it held. And
    A pale fish that used to leap
  For a fly or a grub to the bare

Trees and then sink back to the living water
    Forgot the way : and died in
The dry branches. The baked island was crusted
    With the blue eggs of terns from
    Which no soft wings would ever
    Break to fly in the sun. And the raw

Turtle crawled inland instead of towards the
    Sea, believing the parched soil
Would change to sand again. They thought the killing
    Was over : but the needle
    Had run wild in the shell. The
    Poison was in the salt current of

The world. Let no Jew or Gentile believe that
    The fly in the brain of the
Bald man adjusting his earphones annuls his
    Own nature ; nor pity the
    Man imprisoned for stealing
    Fire from heaven. He,too, is guilty.

I'd say their marble cubicles were a shade
Too small for the taller men, but they all appeared
To be standing at ease. O the usual postures — hands
In their pockets, hands on their hips, hands on the wall.
A few touched themselves. A few were saying prayers
Perhaps. I expect a few were feeling the cold
From that bare cement floor in those bedroom slippers.
I did, in my shoes ; but still, I suppose one allows
A little latitude in the provinces. No money
To do it all in style. However, it worked
And we did get going. One man was reluctant
To co-operate about buttons — a big fellow
With a lot of weight to throw around : it's always
Annoying that sort of thing : a nasty business
It can be on those tiles. So we gave a hand,
Igor and I. The locals didn't mind,
They rarely do. From there it was plain sailing
To the main business. The five attendants came
All according to the book, well-turned-out men
In their new aprons, with the usual hoses, and a good
Flexible pump. (I gave them marks for that. You know
There's a lot of friction on those grids if they scuffle
When you fit the neck-plates.
It might be worthwhile specifying cable,
Steel-strapped stuff ; it would save in the long run.)
Fortunately, we didn't need it : they were all so docile,
Queued and shuffled out with no trouble at all.
Though the line-up was tricky — they'd done the count
   wrong
So we had to use the shoe-horn on a couple.
But after that it was fine : taps on,
Mask fitted, the legs well held, the right grip
And a nice simple injection — I always think
Those gas-cylinders are all wrong. The infusion

Was one of the smoothest I've seen. Evacuation
Very decent. An infinity of freshness
In a little diffusion of bitter carbolic. Rather sweet.
It took about fifteen minutes to get the stories,
And not much mess : they had to scrub the channel
To clear some vomit, otherwise all O.K.
No frills : but at least the operation was completed
With all proper precautions, the doors closed,
The men screened : and, O yes, the windows open
To clean the air. I doubt if anyone smelled
A rat in the whole building, or heard as much
As a squeak from a plimsoll. They moved like pro-
    fessionals
From start to finish. I'd say it was all good work.
They certainly do things with the minimum fuss.
I'd recommend we exonerate the whole depot.

DROP

Sky was the white soil you
Grew in. When the fourth stick broke
      Into thistledown
At the crack of a whistle, streaked brown

    From the crutch out with a crust
Of fear it was like an orgasm to
      Fork into air.
I could see why they'd nicked that nylon

    Rip-cord 'the release'. We
Spread like a leprosy on their clean
      Sun to the wogs. You
Could see their screwed heads grow up

    Like dry coal we'd got
To clap a match to. Christ it was good
      To feel the sick
Flap of the envelope in the wind :

    Like galloping under a stallion's
Belly. Half of Africa flushed
      Out and cocked
Up : you could piss in its eye. You could want to

    Scream the Marseillaise like a
Hymn. And then it was all gone.
      Splum. You were sinking
In a hot bog you'd never wrench

    Clear of alive. Soaked,
Vomiting, jelly-marrowed, afraid
      To spit. No life
Left but that leg-breaking drop on a

Split stockade where they'd have your
Genitals off. You were strung up like Jesus
        Christ in the strings
Of your own carriage : lynched by the Kosher

Sluts who'd packed your chute.
It couldn't work. You were on your own.
        The stick had died
In the screws or never dropped. When the ground

Slammed you at eighteen feet
Per second you were out skedaddling for the first
        Tree with your harness
Cut : the sten jammed whore-

hot yammering out of your
Groin. You were implementing the drill
        Balls : it was flog
On till you blacked out dead.

THE DISCIPLE

I wore a black band. I thought
They would crucify Him in jail. The
Word broke from His agony in the cells. I
Awoke transfigured by incarnate
Will. When He walked out alive I knew
That He was our Saviour. I remember His
Burned face sharp in a nimbus
Of blurred light against the taut flags when He spoke

To our massed lifted hands at
The Rally. I knelt chilled by the bare
Marble before the fed flame for His dead
Martyrs. I knew in my caught heart we
Must all repeat His suffering. I
Wept the oath. I was dedicated to the
Stern commitments of a snapped
Order. I swore to purify my blood of

Evil. I accepted the
Fires of hell on earth. Each uniform
I wore was as my flesh. Its coarse fibres were
Burned by Evil, scraped bare of dust of
Evil, encrusted with excrement
Of Evil. I breathed Evil in the stench of
The bean soup we drank, the bags
Of charcoal I unheaped for the furnaces,

The pit of my soul. When I
Raked the ovens or even touched a
Spade I felt sick. I vomited when I saw
The pyramid of their bodies for
The first time. When a crying child stretched
Out her arms to me I was moved to sweep her
Clear of the doors. I was not
A strong-willed man. I fought to do the hard thing

Well but the Evil within
   Me fought back. I lay awake hearing
Them scream. I committed the sin of pity
   For Evil every time I touched
Their brittle limbs. In my dreams I was
Watching my infant sister crawled on by stick
      Insects with human faces.
Gas was like incense : it drowned corruption. In

      The wind or in cylinders
   To be raised and used it became a
Presence more real than His. Above my bed
   His tense eyes looked down while I slept and
Forgave or condemned. His enormous
Words on the air proved that He still existed
      And surely cared : but I held
A scarred ikon close to my heart which showed Him

      Massacred in the streets by
   The Blood of Evil. I walked in the
Foul heresy of admiring His weakness
   More than His rise to power : but I
Groped my way back. The laceration
Of conscience began to ease. And the toil of
      Confronting the Evil in
Others began to confront the Evil in

      Me. I was helped. I confessed
   My doubts. I endured the controlling
Speech and hands of those more sure in their faith than
   I. And by Grace I recovered my
Sanity and was purified in
Body and spirit. Behind a locked door in
      A blaze of light on a plain
Slate floor my schism was healed by the salt of

Fear. I have no stain left to
Scour. I cut into your wire a saved
Man. I am freed from sin by the mechanism
Of holy justice. I heard of His
Death as if the meaning of Life had
Been for a moment suspended but felt no
Grief. I have shed my heavy
Cross and abide my end in peace of spirit.

ST ANDREW'S

Here in my tight suit, Sunday after Sunday,
I'd shiver in the draughty oblong hall.
(The fire-bomb-gutted church was never used
Except by children or for some church play
That needed ruins.) Here my pimpled skin

Wrinkled in prayer when I propped my head
On my poised fingers : forms of words worn thin
Helped me to remember what should be said.
I'd bend beside my mother, gangling, tall.
I prayed for faith, but felt that God refused.

Let me look back. I'm there in my rough chair,
Bare legs on sharp straw, sucking buttermint
Slipped in my fidgeting hands by fur-gloved hands.
I'm wondering when the intercession-prayer
Will end. More prayers, intimations, hymns

Flounce leisurely on. I watch bulged offering-bags
Shuttle between deacons. Touched coins chink. Stiff
    limbs
Ease. The soft mouths, whose belly-velvet sags,
Gape for warmed silver, trickling out by dint
Of pressed appeals for 'our missions in far lands'.

The lesson booms out. James McClusky's black
Bony razor-headed bust above the bible
Strops his Highland vowels. Quick Scottish wives
Nudge their slumped husbands. Folded arms, feet slack
On loud planks correct themselves. The Book

Quietly shuts, gold leaves flutter. Towards
The back of the hall the text from Habbakuk
Re-echoes. The draped lectern's tasselled cords
Jerk to swung robes. The minister turns : the table
Quakes to beat fists condemning our distracted lives.

Let me look forward. As I grate on boards
I bump the lion-mouthed mahogany throne
He'd hunch in. It's ground by lecturers now. Dead flowers
Droop on the flat piano from which the Lord's
Thundering praises were wrung. I cough and choke

In dust (it's little played now) and stoop through
To the new church : too elegant in oak
For my taste. I advance to our old pew
Through pipe-warmed air. I sit down, scrape fresh stone
With dragging nailed heels. Here, while quarter-hours

Flake from the tower, I stop. My child's belief
(I now believe) was a Scots exile's ; gone
With loosened roots. When the sick wish returns
For the lost country, the dream-Scotland grief
Was noble in, I clutch at *things*, plain things

I've lifted to symbols : compasses, a brooch,
Photographs, draughtsman's T-squares, opal rings.
My faith's planted where prayers can't encroach.
I've grown past God-roots. Why, then, back there on
That warm pew do they prick me ? Something turns

Time back. It's Easter Day. I see moved plates
Of diced white bread, starched linen someone clears.
The plates clink closer. Furtively, I choose
Christ's body and blood. The hushed young elder waits,
Then catfoots on. And now I'm swallowing wine

From a glass thimble, rolling the lifeless bread
On my living tongue, I'm keyed for some sure sign
Of something miraculous. Eyes blink ; my head
Lifts ; and I stare at grown men shedding tears
And my own goosefleshed knees, blue with a bruise.

A RITUAL

I walk there with a book : along a street
    Where dust is settling, rinsed with rain,
And small cars honk and weave, delivering meat
    Through carts and vans : then past a wall
Filled in with windows, where men laugh and eat.

It's always lunch-time. I glide in through doors
    Of warm plate-glass, nod to a tall
Hall porter, pad past stairs to other floors,
    Turn, and again read, blocked on board,
The plain red word with its rich hint of wars,

Blood-donors, and queue up to wait my turn.
    Here women grin, fidget, look bored.
Men read or smoke. None speaks. A nurse looks stern,
    Wheeling a cripple past. I sit
Staring at someone's trousers where a burn

Has scorched them brown. I read. It tells, in verse,
    How people lose the power to spit
When they feel fear. I edge towards the nurse
    Whose cards possess me. In my head
I dream I have her, but she has the curse.

They always do. She takes my hands, pricks in
    A needle, samples blood. Slow, red
And steady it comes through the severed skin
    And stains the glass. I sign my name
To swear I've not had jaundice, bark my shin,

Wink at the doctor, clutch my bottle, go.
    The next room's very much the same.
More waiting. Coats off, sleeves rolled this time. No
    Attempts to read. Across the room
Others have started, lying row by row

As we shall soon be. Then it's me. Flat, neat,
   Below my head I feel the tomb
I lay my grey crusader's coat on. Feet
   Together, arms at sides, I lie
Watching the fan slash, feeling like white meat.

Another doctor looms. White face. White hands.
   Then biting questions: how? when? why?
And round my arm, cool, tight, stretched cotton
     bands.
   A vein swells: the heart-gauge records
Its pressure, and a vampire nurse who stands

Ready to put the tube in, grips my fist
   Around a small pot barrel. Swords
And hot steam, Romans dying, wrist by wrist,
   Blur in the fan revolving. Then
The needle jabs. I feel the burst skin squist,

And start to squeeze. It all comes out at last
   If you go on. Of course, some men
Prop their heads up—girls' legs don't cross so fast
   Flat out: but most eyes the fan draws
Into its dream, its whirlpool, of the past

Where things could mean more. Making love. Or
     race
   And friends. Or fighting for some cause
Worth being killed for. Blood moves in my face
   And in the glass. I sense the taste,
Like wine, of it. I squeeze on, hold the pace

They told me to, then hear the nurse return.
   I feel her break the tube off, paste
Plaster across the wound. She shows concern
   By smiling, and suggests I rest.
They always do. Time after time I learn

The way to swing down, pick my coat up, walk
    Into the side-room, swing up, test
My lump for size, and lie, drained white as pork
    For seven minutes. Then the tea,
A chocolate biscuit, and a time for talk.

It leaves us then. We all sit round and score
    About the weather. And I see
That lifted body we were monstrants for
    In that far room, three feet away,
Paled to a thin brown trickle, hiss and pour

From a tin spout : and shaken like a tide
    The blood run on its iron tray
Into the blood-starved wood that stirs inside,
    Which we must quit soon, hot and well,
Knowing we answered when its raw throats cried.

A CHRISTMAS RING

I

The Conception

On the first day of Christmas, when it snowed,
I lounged indoors, lulled by mulled wine, and read.
Then, I envisaged these sonnets, in a mode
Intricate as mah jong. Monk-like, I sought what thread

I ought to sew with. Well, Biafra was owed
A delicate needle's care : some would have said
I ought to salute the Jordan, as it flowed
With blood, or see the starved in Christ were fed.

I know. It seemed an abuse of care to write
Only for Chinese pleasure, to pare time
In a warm room, seek themes out, switch on light,

And note swirled snow braking. Englazed in rhyme,
So much rang false. I heard the screech-owl creak,
Strafing each flake, immigrant to his beak.

II

The Pilgrimage

Strafing each flake, immigrant to his beak,
A stiff gull swooped. Light swanned along the lawn
On the second day of Christmas, glassily meek
Through snow-feathers. After a shepherd's dawn

Streaked in the East, a sheepish wind strayed, piq-
uant, smoke-filled. As I passed an oak-stump, sawn
For fire-wood in the park, it crossed me, reek
Of dried thorns burning. Was it meant to warn ?

A slush dome stretched in close, mist-ridden grey
Across England. Air changed. I felt it flay
My nostrils, eyes blear, feet slurred loose and slowed.

Suddenly, there were defences for this form.
A crisp sound echoed. Shanghaied through the storm,
A blackbird scattered his incense in the road.

III

The Annunciation

A blackbird scattered his incense in the road,
Welcoming me home. From communion blood I came,
Just before twelve, to my cleared snow. He showed
A blue-shot wing, and a bill of desperate flame,

As I stamped by him. Work slumped like a toad
On the third day of Christmas. I felt lame,
Hung-up, and guilty. Pride would need a goad
To start me composing, but this bird was game.

I set the pierced Yale to the jagged lock
And coughed indoors. The cold air zipped my brain.
Christ, it was that cat from next door again.

Look out, there, bird. As if to break my block,
With slow blows, he divided his gold Word. *Eeek!*
Max leapt to extol him, with a grief-hewn cheek.

IV

The Milk

Max leapt to extol him. With a grief-hewn cheek
On the fourth day of Christmas, dipping pots
In the cream of human kindness, as all week,
Our milkman smiled. Max camouflaged his spots.

O, Max is very sweet. Would never seek
To kill the Christ. Why, he licks babes in cots,
Is always gracious, gentle. Quite unique
Among the cats one knows, in knowing what's

What. Well, I see Max has one key to life,
Tuning his belfry of hunger, fly deceit,
And brazen for what he knows. He nudged my wife

Tenderly, filched some milk, then turned his feet
And tailed off. Life was a Ming episode,
Extending paws by water, where some flowed.

V

The Waste

Extending paws by water, where some flowed,
Max made me think of Asia. Near his drain,
I watched the waste rush. As he mewed and toed,
Life seemed a war. In Vietnam, as in Spain,

On the fifth day of Christmas, bombs would explode,
Rice straw burn, girls be raped, men slain,
And cats tease birds, and kill them. A cock crowed
For pagan Max in that red-spattered rain

Of soup, and tea, and peelings. Devilish, he
Savaged the gods in Bangkok, gulped the sea.
All flesh was grass. Each Himalayan peak

Melted in milk. Max hunched, then sprang at leaves,
Leaving me shaking blood-stock from my sleeves,
Hard by the drain-cope, red-specked from a leak.

VI

The Visitor

Hard by the drain-cope, red-specked, from a leak
A spider staggered. Along snow-swept stones
He stalked, circled in glory, as a freak
Ordained by nature. In my flu-stiff bones

I felt health squelching. Once, to some frail Greek,
He might have seemed a portent, fit for tones
Of grave thanks, weighty gnomes. I felt too weak
For such pre-Christian versing. Near the Nones,

All beasts were soporific. Awe-struck, ill
On the sixth day of Christmas from a chill,
I chose to praise a thrawn one, whose abode

Was a house of darkness. Flushed from pipes to work,
He swayed through waste. Eight legs blurred, vague in
  mirk
Where the tired crab-apple cleared its load.

VII

The Agony

Where the tired crab-apple cleared its load
Our hedgehog used to feed. Last summer, one
Night, as we talked in darkness, and heat mowed
And swept the terrace, I heard something stun

Stone, claw on concrete. By some branch's node
A strong foot seemed to grip. I thought, in fun,
Of Pindar's athletes. Then, as in an ode,
We found one squatting, quilled, and poised to run.

Well, on the seventh day of Christmas, milk
Might have been spread, with sogged bread, silk
In texture, and he might have stubbed home sleek.

That summer midnight he was carved in fear,
Hearing an owl. Today, from somewhere near,
I heard Christ's agony in the garden shriek.

VIII

The Crucifixion

I heard Christ's agony in the garden shriek
On the eighth day of Christmas, from his box,
Where he was coughing blood. A thorn-shaped streak
Of wet had mussed his back-fur. Muffled shocks,

Guns, firing on some serial, smoothed and chic,
Super-charged the horror. Listening clocks
In all the rooms made living seem oblique.
This was the killing-hour. Some came in smocks

37

With hammers, others with green liquids, wires,
And it was easy. All were penned, and killed.
Some by the crucifix, some trapped, and filled

With pheno-barbitone. A row of pyres
Blazed. I was where a small one's corpse was tossed.
Above his fur, snow-grey, the New Year crossed.

IX

The Resurrection

Above his fur, snow-grey, the New Year crossed,
As Max walked out, and stroked things with his tail,
On the ninth day of Christmas. Coffin-mossed,
I dreamed about slain Peter. Like a snail,

I grieved a trail of glair for what was lost,
And made a wreath of shadows. Nail by nail,
I felt his box assembled, and embossed
With Christian fish. Outdoors, in sudden hail,

The garden flushed and rattled. Through a mist,
It seemed that there were green slides moving in
A sort of broken halo of red light.

I looked and wished. The watch-hands at my wrist
Shone for my cat, and all his living kin,
As, near its child, that nail-bright star by night.

X

The Love

As, near its child, that nail-bright star by night,
So, in the morning, through a muggy fog
On the tenth day of Christmas there shone light
On Tabitha. She lay dumb, like a dog,

Along my Indian carpet, striped and slight,
Near to the fire. In her cat's catalogue
Few qualify, save Max. Max, in her sight,
Is as a brother, as he is. No clog

38

Sits closer to its foot, than Max to her.
She leaned, and slicked her tongue along his fur,
In Christian love. As Max rose, being Max,

And cuffed her, she cuffed him, then both made pax.
Writing, I smiled. Max cavorted, grey on white
Over the ice. On crisp leaves, Max trod light.

XI

The Ministry

Over the ice, on crisp leaves, Max trod light
On the eleventh day of Christmas. Near the flats,
Leaping, he sprayed. I laughed, and thought of tight,
Immaculate forms. If cats were all grey mats

On which to balance Chinese thoughts, one might
Spray to Confucius. Well, such spotless cats
As please the Lord must simulate his flight,
And rise to heaven. If men die like rats

In war and famine through the world, is verse,
Infected with such chronic cat-flu, worse
Than silence, prose ? Well, what if it's not true

That a slash of cruel headlines nails you through ?
Suppose, though, a brittle corpse does, burned, and
    tossed
Across a bald earth, graved in pewter frost ?

XII

The Contrition

A cross, a bald earth. Graved in pewter frost,
On the twelfth day of Christmas, a girl came
To beg for Oxfam. For so small a cost,
How could I jib at helping ? All the same,

Here was a hard sell. I felt pushed and bossed
Against my natural wax. I let the flame
Gutter along my cold staff, die enfossed,
And closed the door. Is, Murder, then, my name?

O, dear. To talk of writing because art
Means somehow coping, and then shrink from coins
Veiled in a box! Eating, I shivered. Sleet

Had been along the window, making part
More clean. Max came today, and coiled his loins
Near to where Tabitha strayed, smokily neat.

XIII

The Betrayal

Near to where Tabitha strayed, smokily neat,
Her brother hunted. In my pine, a bird,
The same that scattered incense, woke to the cheat
Of a warm day. As to the risen Word

In all His Glory, you could hear Max bleat,
Fleeced before March. In wolfskin boots, and furred,
He leapt be-knighted. As the ear to wheat,
Christ was a roaring flame. Deprived, Max heard

His clapper of derision ring loud and clear
Hosannas to the heights. Max had been near
To what he thought a special New Year's treat.

He purred in rage. Fingering down cards, I saw
Tabitha enter, gentle with tooth and claw
Under chrysanthemums. I heard Christ's wings beat.

XIV

The Entombment

Under chrysanthemums, I heard Christ's wings beat
When he fell black from heaven. On the ground,
Missionless, he was only so much meat
On a bird's bones. Where was that amber sound

40

That scorched the air, and hung there, like the heat
Of the last furnace? Finished, in their mound,
October's thorns lay frozen. Down the street,
Starting, a jaguar rasped, rasped. Like a round,

I felt my poem snarl towards its end,
Swallowing Christ's wings. At Easter, would they bend
In restless flying? To Tabitha he seemed

Motionless feathers. As she lay and dreamed,
I saw grey flakes, braking to stall, implode
On the first day of Christmas, when it snowed.

XV

The Glory

On the first day of Christmas, when it snowed,
Strafing each flake, immigrant to his beak,
A blackbird scattered his incense. In the road,
Max leapt to extol him, with a grief-hewn cheek,

Extending paws by water, where some flowed
Hard by the drain-cope. Red-specked from a leak,
Where the tired crab-apple cleared its load,
I heard Christ's agony in the garden shriek.

Above his fur, snow-grey, the New Year crossed,
As, near its child, that nail-bright star by night,
Over the ice. On crisp leaves, Max trod light

Across a bald earth, graved in pewter frost
Near to where Tabitha strayed, smokily neat
Under chrysanthemums. I heard Christ's wings beat.

THE WASPS' NEST

All day to the loose tile behind the parapet
The droning bombers fled : in the wet gutter
Belly-upwards the dead were lying, numbed
By October cold. And now the bloat queen,
Sick-orange, with wings draped, and feelers trailing,
Like Helen combing her hair, posed on the ledge
Twenty feet above the traffic. I watched, just a foot
From her eyes, very glad of the hard glass parting
My pressed human nose from her angry sting
And her heavy power to warm the cold future
Sunk in unfertilised eggs. And I thought : if I reached
And inched this window open, and cut her in half
With my unclasped pen-knife, I could exterminate
An unborn generation. All next summer,
If she survives, the stepped roof will swarm
With a jam of striped fighters. Therefore, this winter
In burning sulphur in their dug-out hangars
All the bred wasps must die. Unless I kill her.
So I balanced assassination with genocide
As the queen walked on the ledge, a foot from my eyes
In the last sun of the year, the responsible man
With a cold nose, who knew that he must kill,
Coming to no sure conclusion, nor anxious to come.

THE BIRD

When I got home
Last night I found
A bird the cat
Had brought into the house
On the kitchen floor.

It wasn't dead.
It looked as if
It was, at first.
There were some feathers lying
Against the wall :

The bird itself
With its wings folded
Lay and stared.
It didn't move.
I picked it up :

Quivering like a clockwork
Toy in my hand
I carried it out
Into the yard
And put it down

In a slice of light
From the door. I lifted
A long broom
By the handle near to
The head and struck

The bird four times.
The fourth time it
Didn't move.
Blood, in a stringy
Trickle, blotched

The white concrete.
I edged the remains
Up with a red
Plastic shovel.
Lifting it through

The house to the cellar
I tipped it out
In the dust-bin along with
Snakes of fluff
And empty soup-tins.

When I emptied the tea-leaves
This morning I saw
The bird I killed
Leaning its head
On a broken egg-shell.

THE DRAWER

Their belongings were buried side by side
In a shallow bureau drawer. There was her
Crocodile handbag, letters, a brooch,
All that was in the bedside cupboard
And a small green jar she'd had for flowers.

My father's were in an envelope:
A khaki lanyard, crushed handkerchief,
Twelve cigarettes, a copying-pencil,
All he had on him when he was killed
Or all my mother wanted to keep.

I put them together seven years ago.
Now that we've moved, my wife and I,
To a house of our own, I've taken them out.
Until we can find another spare drawer
They're packed in a cardboard box in the hall.

So this dead, middle-aged, middle-class man
Killed by a misfired shell, and his wife
Dead of cirrhosis, have left one son
Aged nine, aged nineteen, aged twenty-six,
Who has buried them both in a cardboard box.

THE COMPASSES

Baroque-handled and sharp
With blunt lead in their lips
And their fluted legs together
My father's compasses
Lie buried in this flat box.

I take it out of its drawer,
Snap old elastic bands
And rub the frayed leatherette:
It smells faintly of smoke:
The broken hinges yawn.

As I level the case to look
A yellowed protractor claps
Against black-papered board,
Sliding loose in the lid
Behind a torn silk flap.

I look in the base at the dusty
Velvet cavities:
Dead-still, stiff in the joints
And side by side they lie
Like armoured knights on a tomb.

One by one I lift
Them out in the winter air
And wipe some dust away:
Screw back their gaping lips
And bend the rigid knees.

In an inch of hollowed bone
Two cylinders of lead
Slither against each other
With a faint scurrying sound.
I lay them carefully back

And close the case. In Crookes
My father's bones are scattered
In a measured space of ground :
Given his flair for drawing
These compasses should be there

Not locked away in a box
By an uninstructed son
But like an Egyptian king's
Ready shield and swords
Beside his crumbling hand.

THE RETURN

After the light has set
First I imagine silence : then the stroke
As if some drum beat outside has come in.
And in the silence I smell moving smoke
And feel the touch of coarse cloth on my skin.
And all is darkness yet
Save where the hot wax withers by my chin.

When I had fallen (bone
Bloodying wet stone) he would lead me back
Along the street and up the corkscrew stair
(Time running anti-clockwise, fingers slack)
And open windows to let in fresh air
And leave me stretched alone
With sunken cheeks drained whiter than my hair.

Then I was young. Before
Another stroke he will come back in bone
And thin my heart. That soot-black hill will break
And raise him in his clay suit from the stone
While my chalk-ridden fingers dryly ache
And burn. On this rush floor
He will come striding hotly. When I wake

The stroke will have been tolled
And I shall take his crushed purse in my hand
And feel it pulse (warm, empty) on my wrist.
Blood floods my temples. Clay man, from what land
Have you come back to keep your freezing tryst
With someone grown so old ?
Soldier, forgive me. Candles die in mist.

And now a cold wind stirs
Inside the shuttered room. I feel his hand
Brushing the stale air, feeling for my place
Across the phlegm-soaked pillows. I am sand
Threading a glass with slow and even pace
    And dying in my furs.
My father turns, with tears on his young face.

THE LAND-MINE

It fell when I was sleeping. In my dream
   It brought the garden to the house
And let it in. I heard no parrot scream
   Or lion roar, but there were flowers
And water flowing where the cellared mouse
Was all before. And air moved as in bowers

Of cedar with a scented breath of smoke
   And fire. I rubbed scales from my eyes
And white with brushed stone in my hair half-woke
   In fear. I saw my father kneel
On glass that scarred the ground. And there were flies
Thick on that water, weeds around his heel

Where he was praying. And I knew that night
   Had cataracted through the wall
And loosed fine doors whose hinges had been tight
   And made each window weep glass tears
That clawed my hands. I climbed through holes. My hall
Where I had lain asleep with stoppered ears

Was all in ruins, planted thick with grime
   Of war. I walked as if in greaves
Through fire, lay down in gutters choked with lime
   And spoke for help. Alas, those birds
That dived in light above me in the leaves
Were birds of prey, and paid no heed to words.

Now I was walking, wearing on my brow
   What moved before through fireless coal
And held my father's head. I touch it now
   And feel my dream go. And no sound
That flying birds can make, or burrowing mole,
Will bring my garden back, or break new ground.

The war is over and the mine has gone
That filled the air with whinnying fire
And no more nights will I lie waiting on
Cold metal or cold stone to freeze
Before it comes again. That day of ire,
If it shall come, will find me on my knees.

THE SHELL

Since the shell came and took you in its arms
    Whose body was fine bone
That walked in light beside a place of flowers,
     Why should your son
Years after the eclipse of those alarms
    Perplex this bitten stone
For some spent issue of the sea ? Not one
Blue drop of drying blood I could call ours

In all that ocean that you were remains
    To move again. I come
Through darkness from a distance to your tomb
     And feel the swell
Where a dark flood goes headlong to the drains.
    I hear black hailstones drum
Like cold slugs on your skin. There is no bell
To tell what drowned king founders. Violets bloom

Where someone died. I dream that overhead
    I hear a bomber drone
And feel again stiff pumping of slow guns
     Then the All Clear's
Voice break, and the long summing of the dead
    Below the siren's moan
Subdue the salt flood of all blood and tears
To a prolonged strained weeping sound that stuns.

I turn in anger. By whatever stars
    Clear out of drifting rack
This winter evening I revive my claim
     To what has gone
Beyond your dying fall. Through these cold bars
    I feel your breaking back
And live again your body falling on
That flood of stone where no white Saviour came

On Christian feet to lift you to the verge
   Or swans with wings of fire
Whose necks were arched in mourning. Black as coal
    I turn to go
Out of the graveyard. Headstone shadows merge
   And blur. I see the spire
Lift over corpses. And I sense the flow
Of death like honey to make all things whole.

THE WARD

Along that ward men died each winter night.
    One in an iron lung
Used to cry out before that salving tin
Strapped round his breathing stifled him. One hung
    In a strange brace
That moved his dead leg gently. And no light
    Out of that blaze where Hitler in
His burning concrete died lit the cramped face

Of a boy paralysed. I in that war
    Lay with cold steel on wrists
Recording how my heart beat, saved and one
With the men dying. Dark amidst the mists
    Across the seas
Each night in France those armies gripped and tore
    Each other's guts out, and no sun
Arched in at dawn through stiff windows to ease

Men left in pain. Sisters on morning rounds
    Brought laundered sheets and screens
Where they were needed. And when doctors came
In clean coats with their talk and their machines,
    Behind their eyes
Moving to help, what was there? To the sounds
    Of distant gunfire, in our name,
So many men walked into death. What lies

And festers is the wastage. Here the beast
    Still breathes its burning stone
And claws the entrails. And those hours of cold
When I lay waking, hearing men alone
    Fight into death
Swim back and grip. And I feel rise like yeast
    A sense of the whole world grown old
With no-one winning. And I fight for breath.

THE SON

Her body was all stones. She lay
In the stones like a glass marble. There was
    No moisture in her. There
Was only the dry spleen and the liver
    Gone hard as pumice-stone. I closed

Her eyes. I saw a sole once on
A block of green marble. It was flung straight
    From the living brine, its
Pupils were bright with a strange heat. I watched
    A cat eat it alive. When I

Touched her cheek, the light failed. When I
Moved my open hand on her lips, there was
    No life there. She smelled of
The cheap soap we had washed her in. I saw
    The black hollows below her eyes

Where desire swam. I called her name
In the dark, but no-one answered. There was
    Only the sap rising.
I thought of the clotted mercury in
    The broken thermometer of

Her body. It rose again in
My head to a silver column, a sword
    Of blood in the sun. I
Held to its cross of fire in a dream of
    Climbing. I swam in the air : my

Wings were extended into the
Night. I was borne above the clouds : I flew
    At increasing speeds, to
Increasing altitudes. There was only
    The sun above me. I *was* the

Sun. The world was my mother, I
Spread my wings to protect her growth. She broke
Into wheat and apples
Beneath my rain. I came with my fire to
The sea, to the earth from the air,

To the broken ground with my fresh
Seed. I lay on her cold breast, inhaling
The scent of iris and
Daffodils. There was nothing more to be
Settled. I thought of her dying

Words, how butter would scarcely melt
In her mouth. I heard a wheel squeak and the
Drip of water. I touched
The cold rail and the covering sheet. Your
Light shone in my eyes. Forgive me.

AN ELEGY

Last night I dreamed you came back. In my cot
Of cane I kicked, squat fingers curled like ferns
　　Around your beads. I was just one
And needed things to clutch. Too late one learns
　　(Love passing) all we miss in what
We reach to hold. This morning, in the sun

Along that crowded street, I walked and saw
The ether clear, and your keen face etched through
　　As if on glass. Under the glaze
Of pre-war Kodak in my blood-book, you
　　(As in my mind's eye) pose and thaw
Before my father's hands. In furs you laze

Beside his 30s car with filled-in wheels
While picnic-baskets open. You drink tea
　　On grass. Then by a rock you stand
Staring at sepia water. And with me
　　In tow, throw bread to leaping seals
(That must be Glasgow) smiling. Sun and sand

Open their honeyed vistas, and the war
Swims under water, years away. I turn
　　Pages of pity. Here I sit
With Mac who licked my face when I was born
　　And died for worrying sheep. A door
Into my father's death parts. Here you knit

A fair-isle jersey for him, here link arms
With arms in khaki, here take off his hat
　　And kiss his thin hair. Were you pleased
In this one where you seem to laugh and chat
　　As he drives off ? And what alarms
You in this weirdly blurred one ? Were you seized

By fear or simply dazzled ? There's no end
To all they hint. Each thick page in my brain
    Erupts and bleeds. Rich blood of kin,
Dense with the war, wells upwards like a stain
    Through all my strange thoughts. And no bend
In sleep or waking movement folds it in

Or stops him dying. Blood is in my veins
From things that happened in your body where
    His cool hands touched it, where I lay
Before my birth. In you I climbed a stair
    Whose treads were water, wearing chains
Of ropes of flesh that I was free to fray,

Though not to break. And when my birth day came
I could swing out. And there in light I broke
    And stood bare-naked. I was king
Of all the flowers and sunlight by one stroke
    Of silver blades. I owned his name
And both your blood. Tonight on blood I bring

My anchored body from his broken back
To your thrown side. I count the standing men
    And watch their whispers. Through the door
I hear you weeping. Someone sees me. Then
    They take me in. I sense the crack
In our closed wall and cry for you. Then your

Own time is here. I come to your pale side
And enter in. So many miles of stone
    After that sea I have to walk
Before I reach you ! Why is your clean bone
    So bare ? Has the receding tide
Sucked all your living tissue, left me chalk

Where nothing grows ? No brilliant cells I see,
No poison dew. Death's music plays in green
    On inner ground so often. Growth

Lush as below the sea. Not here. No sheen
   Of dense bloom gathers. That would be
Some bright relief from this blue stone. On both

Sides of your body I confront chalk, find
Only the barren, scentless, tasteless rock
   Of your dry death. So I return
(Dreams passing into day) through glass. I lock
   Your stone wood in my inward mind
And come alive. I feel hot coffee burn,

Laving my throat. I lie on green brocade
Stretched over cane, reflecting. Fifteen hours
   It is since I was in that sleep
Where you were living still. Do any flowers
   Bloom on your grave? I hear a spade
Grate over clay. Years later, I can weep

Only for your belongings: a green jar,
A crocodile-skin hand-bag, a long brush
   That touched your hair. I hold it here
And scrape some living tissue. I could rush
   To tears. I think bereaved men are
Too far at sea in grief for this. How clear

In blood of mind can I be, losing love
At such a distance? Here above your hair
   I know the way to learn. I lie
Broad waking on my cool bed. I am bare
   As he was with you. High above
On this first night I feel wind stroke the sky

And stir my skin. Close by I hear the tune
Of falling rain. And when your body comes
   In gauze like sea-mist from the shore
At morning, I put out my sails from slums
   To clean sea. And below the moon
I enter you in joy, as none before.

DRIVING WEST

I

No, there was nothing first. Only his air
Stretching for ever, as it seemed. And wind
Cool on their dying faces from the hills
Where cars moved through dark forests, bearing gifts
And laughing children to the caves and mines
Far to the West. Where there was pine-scent, wheels
Hung in that air, turning each corner, stilled
On the brink of something.
                    What was clear to see
Lay under lenses, burning in their dream
As they flew in. Bathed in such draughts of blue
As crowned his eyes, in clarity of means,
Awkward for nothing, they began the end
In even patience. And all followed, swift
As had been promised.
                 Then, the summer lake
The war-lord wrote beside, his buttoned coat
Up to his neck, his long eyes evenly
Disposed, flung back the sun.
                      To clapping hands
Each furled his flowered wings. And flowing rain
Came as before, and went, and washed them clean
Of all that blood-fall.

II

               Shielding his thin heart
He drove West as the day died : and the sun
Blazed in his face, clear dazzling like a brass
Cauldron to see the past in, or a gong
Booming with echoes.
               Life was thick with cars

Moving to meet the sea. That summer men
Spent the long draught of gold in going home
To what they loved, the shore. So when it came,
Darkness with all its visors down, it hurt
More than they knew. At first it seemed too bright
For anything but wonder.
                              Low in the sky
The first blow was the blow of light : that night
Its crescent flowered in the East. It cut
Through glass of cars, through heavy walls of stone,
Through skull and fruit. And men like monks in cells,
Bowed on their knees, hands clasped behind their heads,
From zinc-lined solitude were shaken clear
And bathed in darkness. Miles of open light
Swallowed the naked and the lame. From this
No one walked through, and saw.
                                   The second blow,
After such radiance, was the blow of heat
As if an oven opened, or as if
An oven closed.
                   The third blow was the blow
Of blackened wind. No frame of concrete stood
Near to the storm-boss unsplit. Blackened wind
Solid as iron was the mate of flame
And cooled the beaten anvils.
                              When it closed,
Then there was calm. Calm, and the ash. And while
The city rose towards red sky in the East,
Far Westwards like an earthquake in the heart
It felt. Flung forwards by the blast, his head
Broke on the screen. Skin parted, and the blood
Moved in the shape of lightning.
                                  Touched, with eyes
To see with, scarred, he saw. His clothes were stuck
To his back with sweat. Wet, shaking, he lay still,
Racing his head. Then one by one he moved
Ear, nose, lip, jaw, neck, waist, groin, knee, wrist, toe.
He was alive. He rose, then, pressing fists
Into what moved.

                              Miles down the road, past shreds
Of metal with their meat gone, gouged or stayed,
He saw the cans. Pumps fallen, petrol-smell
And air gushing from a gashed tube. *Here, then*,
He thought, *I can live here*. Heaped cans of oil
Shone below stars beside him.
                                        So he turned
And fell head foremost to the gushing air
As the sun rose. And while it climbed in blue
He slept, marked with his blood.
                                        And as he dreamed
Under the draught of air, his mind flowed out
And far down to the wells of darkness. Once
A short man with an axe beside a stream
Butchered a calf, and in the dream its heart
Fell on the grass, and crawled. Another time
Around a castle men who moved like pines
Grew to a noose that strangled. Old, asleep,
Washing slow hands in water, she was there,
Grey-haired and guilty, waiting for their thumbs
To choke her blood and stone.
                                        Then he woke up,
Screaming : and, waking, head askew on cans
Of spilled oil, counting minutes, hearing wind
Sigh in the sunlight, knew that withering stone
Had caused her first death.

                                III

                        He drove back through blood,
Thinking of her. And as he drove things changed :
Noon-light to evening, there was nothing left,
Only a world of scrap. Dark metal bruised,
Flung soup of blood, anchors and driven screws :
The whole dead sea of wrecks lining the road
Emptied his mind. Ship after painted ship
Thrown into crumbs. He drove through nothing, dazed,
Awake, and dreaming.

   62

Burning to the East
Where the city burst and scattered its fine seeds
Into the lap of air, the fires had died.
Only the veins, the main straight roads bored in,
Bordered by drifts of dust. Life thinned from stone
Through grit to powdered ash.

                      So he drove on,
Knowing his quest was meaningless and blank,
Towards what might have been. Then, by a curve
Where the road narrowed, as it should have done,
He parked the car, got out, and went on foot
To where she might have died.

                      There was no sign
Of even iron or fireclay. Stooping down,
He reached out his right hand to brush the dust
And part some, delicately, where she used
To part his hair. As if in sand he stroked
The shape of something in the dust, some shape,
And touched his eyes.

                      Then he stood up, and took
A new coin from his pocket. With his heel
He dug a flat hole, flung it in, and scraped
The ash back over it, speaking aloud,
Or meaning to, these words : *where we lived first,*
Below our window, when they changed the house,
Workmen found coins. They proved its date, showed pride
Of earlier workmen for their blood-fall. Here
I show the same, where there is nothing. Only
The ceremony remains.

                      And then he drove
Out of the dust-bowl, and across the plain
Back towards his refuge, and his cans of oil,
All that the war had brought him, and forgot,
Or tried to for a little, what had died,
Having done all he could.

IV

           Then, as before
That spear-flash in the evening, most were sick
And needed blood, knowing they all were doomed
As she was.
         Awake under buckled steel,
After what lapse of hours she stirred and moved
Still in the tunnel. There was no more light,
No train movement. Somewhere a faucet dripped
Water, blood, water on stone. Inside her brain
The blood beat back.
           Fire was the sign of blood.
After the first blow it returned and beat
Over and over at those broken doors.
It oozed from coal-trucks in a rush of blue-
gold, yellow as gas here, mustard-sharp.
They smelt it coming. Acrid hint of smoke
Under carriage-cloth. Rake of hot-iron heat
Flaring on cheeks. And then that fast-back lick
Of its long tongue, flickering through each crack
In plastered skin and bone, liquid like knives
Cutting and salting. Wincing in its wounds
The whole train split like stitches.
             Men fought with tins
For knives to open tins. Bone-wounds from strikes
In the long club-war of survival healed
And left them hobbling. Over all that fire
Waiting to burst its banks and bleed them dry
They crouched like hens.
          There leather creased and wore
Around low shoulders that were scarred with hawks
From earlier wars. Where in the wall men burned
For being nothing, thunder and leaves were borne
With songs of triumph. Wrenched from these, and oiled,
In coats of black too seared with flame to cool,
Some walked and ruled. Walked when the last cars broke
And there was no more fire. In wars for this,
And pride, over the brick-waste they patrolled,

Circling like rooks. And when they found, they killed :
Or cured what insolence was left, ingrained
From scoured-out power, in pain.
                              Stumbling on rails
Towards that ring of sun, past sweating walls,
Or in her mind, as he had done, she moved
To that church, where she was due.

V

                              There by the grave
Beside slow falling clay she stood in dirt
And watched their heavy faces. Brass and lead
Had stamped their moulds in blue eyes and in brown
Before it happened. Under bells that speared
The cold larks in the clouds, the feuding clans
Blackened the day with grieving.
                              Far away
She saw the cows come downhill to cold farms
And feed on warm hay. Breathless, she recalled
A tight sow with her farrow in her skin
Scraping a nest of sticks for him to fall
And come alive in.
                              Waxed clay into clay,
The passage was performed. The oiled ropes ran
Under and over. And bronzed lion-masks
Amazed the worms.
                              Men coughed and stamped. And bones
Long bearing stress of birth were spared and fell
Into the space below the world they penned
Her glassy eyes in.
                              In earth, in wood and stone,
The coffin-shape lay where it rested. One
Bowed in his hands, tears falling. Hard as ice
He was a winter cave where water flowed
Through aeons of slow time. The other stood
Seeing the keels beach in a sea-weed blaze
Along the Western shore-line.

C   65

                              Layer on layer
The dwindling pyramid of the dead bled in
Over their faces. Red with heat of kin
After the cold earth, by the common grave,
They saw it coming.
                              Beyond her wrecked train
Outside that warring town she felt the chill
Take hold of her.
                              That history of men
Marching with axes over these bared fields
Heraldic now at mid-day, mailed her brain
In heavy chains.
                              She sniffed, and felt hard rot
Smeared like an ointment, strangely thick and sour
Against her skin, ash-breath of coming death
Among the old. Old as they all were old
And he would soon be.

VI

                              Up the mourning stairs
All the white dogs turned round their eyes and frowned
As he came on. The cases creaked and stirred
With what was in them. Silence of clear glass
Behind which all the world could hold its breath
Until the moment came to scream, shivered
And knew its hour.
                              Holding that corpse in mind
The hall was taut with waiting.
                              Then blood broke
Over each surface it had oiled before
In even violence. Absolving red,
Crackling with iron spikes, it struck and spilled,
Swilling jet-metal. Cold wood shook and peeled
Under such pressures that the whole house bulged
Like a bag of water. Willy-nilly, walls oozed
Thick drops, then, blotched with patches, bleached
One even red. What was a refuge once
Wilted to a grave.

That night for the first time
Under one roof, sheltering from their grief
With port and ham, the cousins met. Like a dog
Blood ran between them with its nose to the ground
Sniffing for a scent. One slapped his covered sides
With a brace of gloves like a killed pheasant. One
Hunched his dead side, slurring his vowels like
A load of stone. What there was left to say
Under that flood of grieving no one knew
Except through money. Making, moved by, coins :
This was their only link. Hands shook that shook
Each other's hands. One with his stomach-wound
From alcohol, one rigid from the stroke
Of what had struck him as a child. Each merged
With the sores of Nature.
                         Outside, through blood, the kilns
Burned in the distance, and the bricks were fired,
Squared moulds for men, each holed with a dish. Men
   stoked
The rain-slaked furnaces with coke. Men scarred
Ledgers with ink. These were the fields of war
Where lines of men, black figures, marched and fell
Into the red of death. Hungry or old,
Some lay beneath bricked urns they built and sold
Miles from the houses they put up and bought
All beside slag, soot sifting down through clouds
Of massed rain.
                 And that night the Eastern ash
Gathered and swayed them to the gulf of war
Where all were game-soup. So the cousins met
Behind the kilns, under that night of blood,
Dying, and proud. And no-one spoke, or knew
How they could speak.
                       Her father sat alive,
Dreaming of horses. It could come again,
Come once, and still his guts, they said, would hold
For a year and a day. If he could smoke and play
The bricks could scatter. There were colours, odds
Of another win. So he lay back in tweeds

Beside her cairn, drinking his wine. *Here, then,*
Here's something for you, here, he said.
                                        Then blood
Broke in her dream, as dams break in the brain
To flood the cells. She dreamed of men and guns,
Keys jangling in a tiled hall, and a race
For broken glass. And then it all began
To merge in dazzling anguish of hot lights
Gashing the dark, gushing on walls.
                                        Coughing,
Tossing on red sheets, weeping in her dream,
She knew the end was near. She touched her hair
And felt grey rain turn into hail, white snow,
And cried for him.

VII

                        And as he drove he heard,
And stopped the car, and came to where she was,
Far in, still in the tunnel, blocked, alive
Behind her shattered glass. Her locked hands moved
Like brooched snakes round a cup. There cold red wine
Swirled like his blood. Her burned legs spread, she looked
Ready for death. He kissed her, touched her arms
Gashed to the wrists with red. Her knitted scars
Wove them a skin.
                        Far East the city fell
Into itself. Welded in white heat, fused
Under that hanging sword, they grew as one,
Her cold pearl coming to his shell-bred hands
In milk and scent of musk.
                                That second night,
Sleeping with her, he dreamed his father came
And frowned above him. Wearing black and mud,
He drew high pillars. Coal burned in his eyes
And beams collapsing choked him. Wind and sea
Broke through the hall they talked in, till they drowned
In flowers. Clematis, dark spider, touched
His cold face with her seven hands. He smiled

In his own garden once again. She moved,
His mother, shearing blooms. He was a child,
Married and dying in his mother's arms
Far from the war.
                    And then at noon he woke
With her dead in his arms. She who had lived
Yards from the blast, though miles beyond the blaze,
Dazed with the air had sickened. And so he
Lifted her up, and held her in his hands,
Her black hair falling.
                    Then his walk began
Back to the light-ring and the drifting ash
That would drown him soon, too. Toiling on rails,
Cracked up, he reached the pocked air. Hard and thin
His new breath came. He turned. And as the sun
Sank in the sky, he felt the poison stir
And knew the end was near. Starting his car
He drove on West, the ash-light in his eyes
Glazing the skin with gold. As in his grave,
Wearing his death-mask, he moved into dark
Behind the wheel.
                    And as he drove he seemed
To wake and dream. Two knights lifted their swords,
One with a hawk on his left hand. His feet
Sloughed the rough dust as though on skis in snow
Near to his mountains in the East. Across
That blazing sea, beside his level bay
From which the coarse earth rises, the long port
Waited for his return.
                    And the other came
Short-necked and dark-haired, who had burned his palm
With a slow match. And looking to the light
Above the chair he lay in, stared and slept,
Though waking, to resist the pain. These two
Moved in his dream as he drove on and felt
The poison stirring.
                    So the sun went down
And the car moved on into the Western dark
Nearer and nearer to the sea. Those cans

Of lost oil lay behind, missed long ago
Like her, and their slow burial of the blood,
In gathering black. He heard no horn, no drum,
Only the waves breaking towards the shore
His headlamps bored at. And the gentle ash,
Feather of pity, settled in the wind,
Swirling to fill the earth.
                          So he drove on,
Wading in blood. And, as before and since.
The crown was lifted, and he sank to sleep
In darkness.

VIII

                    And so driving in his dream
He reached the last beach. And the waves washed in
Over the waste sand where no others were
Except his past. There with his wooden spade
And coloured pail he walked along the wall
Searching for where to build. And where the sea
Came to its highest mark below the road
He made her mausoleum.
                          The war of coins
Boiled to a cream of spume. Here all that blood
He bathed and came from soaked his grains with salt
And filled the shifting turrets.
                          Far away
Furled in their fresh cocoons the butterflies
That broke the city slept. And bowls of tea
Passing from hand to hand confirmed the signs
Moving in open pages, quaint and fine.
Their line continued. Pictures in the wind
Sailed into water.
                          And on Western sand
Where he was dying the sharp water leapt
And seethed over the moat, sinking away,
As his dark royal blood sank, through all time.

TO EURYDICE IN HELL

I

Then Orpheus walked in a dark
forest of books and people
thinking of nothing, but

when Eurydice came the leaves
paused on the trees
to listen, the wet snail

cocked its horn, it was
morning everywhere
in the pulsing wood

he called pleasure and
the sun shone. To be stones
rolling in dark brooks

was a new beginning and
dead things broke into flower.
So Orpheus sang.

II

But Eurydice walked in
a close alliance with
nothing, that watched

her. Only the song
of Orpheus could make
her real, and that not

for long. For nine days
the bad core of Eurydice
rotted, but on the tenth

c•

Eurydice died,
and the whole inside of
her moved into hell

where she lay as naked as
nothing. Only
the flesh of Eurydice stayed

alive. And the nothing within her
came out and gashed its name
in her belly, that

bled for Orpheus. Take
away the bones, there is
nothing to hold

Eurydice. Take away
the skin, she has no passport
for the lonely wood

where Orpheus sings. Praise
her in razor-blades, it is
only through pain that

brings pleasure that
sad Eurydice lives now.
So Orpheus sang.

III

Then Orpheus came into hell, who
had no love for the mad
and hated the blind silence

there. And the darkness
reached out its arms
and wrapped Orpheus too

in its chloroform. And he spoke
with dread mud and
water to let

her go. Prayed to
the hot bands in the wall
that they might

leave her. Hands are a spoiled
nuisance, they
pull the soul out. Stay

away, Orpheus, here there is only
the rule of nothing. Eurydice
has gone into skin, she is

no one here. Look.
There is no one here.
So Orpheus sang.

IV

Alas, there is only
tomorrow the black
nowhere to go in

now, is that
it ? Walk, Orpheus, by
the sounding Thames. Your head

the black nurse struck
from your future sticks
like a heart

in the hospital, you
have no brain now
for the world you live

in, it bleeds
in the cold river
Eurydice has dissolved into

you call hell. But look, Orpheus,
Eurydice is a star
whose face kisses your

bloody lips in the
water. You two are
at one now, in the sky.

So Orpheus sang,
believing nothing,
to Eurydice in hell.

THE BLADE

I see her walking on the lawn in white,
  Her feet bare in the ground.
Above her in her room her joss-sticks burn
Rich in an air that lives with dying sound.
I watch hot smoke surround her in the light
    As in an urn.

Then she is writing, and I watch her write,
  Her hand bare on the sheet.
Against her window she has found a bat
That beats its wings to breaking in the heat
To be let in. I watch her toes grow tight
    On the straw mat.

Then she is walking, and I see her pause,
  Her face bare in the glass.
Above her arm I see the raven blue,
Its gouged holes ready for the thing to pass
And let her go. I watch her touch the doors
    No light comes through.

Then I am reading, and I smell the blood,
  Her words bare in my hand.
Then she is talking, and I read her talk
In open purple on a folded band
Where ink has whipped and curdled into mud
    I start to walk.

Then I am with her in the razored air,
  Her tongue bare in my lips.
Under her black thin silks I touch the blade,
Hearing the cracked sink spit where water drips.
Then, where the first light comes, I kiss her hair
    And wake afraid.

THE AVOCADO PLANT

Where you were planted, clouds hung low and grey
Over the clinic roof. She was too sick
   To dig your stone deep. No thin ray
Of quick sun pierced her locked room. Moist and thick
In claustrophobic darkness you grew strong
      And stretched. Those long

Drooping and furrowed leaves, clasped round your stem
And leaned against her peeling walls now, swept
   Up in confined space. Choked with phlegm,
She coughed in cloying heat you throve on, wept
In dry air. Now she grows through barren light
      Where you hang, tight

In all your cells, green leaves turned ashen-grey
And spoiled by wax. Where candles tint her air
   She lies, white-naked. Far away,
Glass-clear in distance, she can hear the flare
Of open gas-jets. Turning to the wall
      I feel her fall

Into my present, and my skin. Her hand
That moves in even silence, twitches, grips
   And stirs the dark scent. She is fanned
Across far water by the wind on lips
She parts on cloth. You die beside her, dark
      As she was dark

In those deep months of nothing. Now the light
In this dense flat, half-open to the sun,
   Rasps your cold skin. You cry for night
For your rough fruits. Your children, one by one,
Falter, are picked. I touch one with my tongue
      In secret, stung

By such bared harshness. Acid in the mouth
You are, dark plant. And in the groin too hard
    For her. I feel her breathe. Far South
Of here you flowered once. As soft as lard
Your dark flesh felt then. Raped of your last stone
        You die alone

Now in the light. Across her flustered bed
She reaches with her finger to your soil
    And stirs your roots. She who has shed
All of her fever in the flex of oil
Lets her hair fall across your leaves. Her breath
        Quickens your death.

THE HEIR

I took him in. One winter night
The wheels we hired were stayed on wet stone. Light
Flared in the stucco. Silent on the stair,
   Linked arm in arm, we rose
As warm air in our crowded house to where
The high room in the darkness held and froze

   White head to head. There, cool in sheets
That smelt of man-sweat, stripped of all my heats,
I lay in rustling, tasting mint and wine
   From his long tongue, and with his hand
Soft on my rough skin, felt his naked spine
And then his groin move, and my shoulder fanned

   By dry hair brushing me. Then rain
Broke on the windows, broke, and broke again
In hissing spikes at war with wrinkling tin
   My flesh was heir to. Trembling, tense,
I lay in my thin sheath, locked in a skin
Too scarce to keep the storm out. Every sense

   Whimpered for pity. I could hear
The bat-squeal, smell the owl-spit, taste the clear
Blood of the mice that split between the claws
   I touched. But what I saw was bone
White on the ground where corpses, fouled with straws,
Worked on each other. So I took one stone

   Out of the hail that washed and filed
My attic window, and I made this child
To lie in flesh so rich with pleasure, blades
   Of grass could rake it. Here it lies,
Hard, wrinkled as a dried fruit's. And what shades
It with his body, is the wind that dies.

THE GOOSE-FLUTE

Once very night I would drive home in light
    And play in you. Whenever now
I hear your low voice moan, the coldness comes
Of waves breaking off Dover, and rain drums
    On decks. If I remember how
 Outside your window a dark hand caressed
      And lit that night
When my green wings and branches lay undressed,

I touch your smooth clay, finger your dry beak
    And suck your lips. Then clear notes rasp
Into my ridged mind. I am deep awake
Under your music. In my skin the ache
    Opens again. I touch the clasp
Latching the sea-air of your body. Death
      Puffs out my cheek :
I feel the riving suction of your breath

Driving my braced legs to the brink. I break
    Into thick sweat, not knowing why
I sweat. My wheel-hub shadows flee and loop
Under the wide wings of an owl. One swoop
    Lifts him high over the black sky
And your stretched skin. Are we one flute of bone
      Tuned to the rake
Of these long claws that scar the frigid stone

And spark its fire ? No, the clay stops are legs
    I stroke in you. That yolk of sound
I pulled from cool depths with my lips and tongue
Melts in your belly. Where its yellow swung
    In heavy silence I walk round
And find no way in. Hollow walls of white
      Smooth like an egg's
Arch and are hard, infertile as the night

Outside your four holes. Nowhere do rooms clear
   A view of water. No soft palms
Rear in your desert where the clay and sand
Fragment to nothing. You are locked in land
   Beyond the reach of holy psalms
Played on the wind. These wheels are pitching decks
     That I must steer
Out of your future through a sea of wrecks.

A STAR

     Above the violent park
Where only men with knives walk bright as air
       She drifts in peace
Too rich in light for darkness to make way
   Beyond her screens. No drop of night
Filters through windows where the ice of day
Mingles through mirrors with the muted white
Of all her walls. She moves through golden fleece
Out of the rain, past chair piled high on chair,
      Into the womb of dark,

     Alone. Above the park
I see the flaming oriole of her hair
       Swing like a fleece
Flirting with air. In silent love I sway
   By temples whose cold locks hang tight
Against my fingers that would loose and play
Through all her flames. I taste their burning white
On my raw lash. Alas, there is no peace
Unless I shed her brilliance from my chair
      And lose her in the dark.

     See, where the dying park
Erupts with light ! With knives they strip her bare
       And part her fleece
And lay her in the ground and make their way
   Where no help comes. I sense thick light
Swirl in the windows. The broad fin of day
Swims to the surface. Edged with flirting white
She veers towards me. If I break my peace
And flow to meet her, cool night-scented air
      Will fill the world. Such dark

Has never been. The park
Opens its willows to the morning air
     Where all her fleece
Echos and burns to nothing. Far away
   There comes a sound whose leaves are white
For all her silver cloisters and her sway
Of Southern fire. This is my tree tonight
That listens for the wind within the fleece
And sings in flame. O tree, sing through her hair
    As she sways into dark !

THE DEATH-BELL

I see you enter through the silver door
   Under the tail. To where your throne
Rests in its grooves, you move on naked feet,
Alive, and well. Strapped in, you sit alone.
I see your toes, white worms along the floor,
   Carved as in glass. Our cold eyes meet,

Mine across miles of waiting, as before.
   No, in some lethal under-tone
I sense one difference. You slide your seat
More gently, with your polished knuckle-bone
White on its arm. I hear a strange wind roar
   As you take off, brilliant and neat,

Into the air. I think I feel it more
   Than when it happened. In the drone
Of all that wind, air gathers to repeat
My sense of why. Once it was like a stone
Locked riding in the heart, as in a store,
   And soon to grow, and bloom, like wheat

Beside the sea. My blood-thing, in the core
   Of our green love I heard you moan
Like oceans on the shore, driven by sleet
Against my neck for safety. All I own
Sinks into this : that we are still at war
   And burn like soldiers in the heat.

The sun dies into space. Your bright wings bore
   Holes in the blue. As in a cone
Through which salt drifts and falls, even and fleet,
Your body drifts through silence. Lightly blown
By air from tubes above your head, one spore
   Of what we called love drops, dead meat.

LIVING IN THE ECHO

I see two women, walking
into the darkness away
from me. One
is the one I am losing

now, the other
the one who was lost
in the darkness and
came out.

There is no end, only
the women walking
slowly with bowed
heads into the

darkness, the light
behind, always
behind, and my
own shadow

breaking
over their bodies, the
dark skin
against the light.

PRAYER TO THE WHITE LADY

after Himnusz Minden Idoben
by Laszlo Nagy

I

Creature of flame, out of
the sun's bow I call you :
moment of crystal for the throwing-knife,
  lighten my darkness, I
need you now.

II

O, lady of the small larks,
keeper of the instruments
in the zenith, last room of the king,
  lighten my darkness, I
need you now.

III

Palm in the rain of sorrow,
fire under glaze, lifting
the twin domes of your body above me,
  lighten my darkness, I
need you now.

IV

Mistress of Victory, flame
of the gathering storm, brightening
into the jails of my eyes,
  lighten my darkness, I
need you now.

V

Nurse of the war-wounded, yours is
the house of the Jew and the Negro :
draught of the bee's kiss, mysterious honey,
    lighten my darkness, I
need you now.

VI

Lady, oblivious of blood and money,
belly-dancer of hunger, echo
and resonance of the millennium,
    lighten my darkness, I
need you now.

VII

O, my dear one, tempered
by the beam of the laser, torn
by the stone body of the gorgon, the man-child,
    lighten my darkness, I
need you now.

VIII

Always your tall house was open to me,
glittering with expectation : O, godlike
above the bronze cauldron of your beauty,
    lighten my darkness, I
need you now.

IX

In the beginning I felt your body lap me,
drowning into the saraband of love :
killer of the black crows that haunt me,
    lighten my darkness, I
need you now.

X

Now, on the brink of the vacuum, at the edge
where the million tendrils of nothingness
are erupting, even out of my own mind,
lighten my darkness, I
need you now.

XI

Lady of pain, sharer of this affliction,
sufferer under the same electric coil :
now, as I reach for the dark pill and the needle,
lighten my darkness, I
need you now.

XII

Only in you will the house of my body glisten
gold in all its chimneys and veins :
only in you will the white pigeons flicker,
lighten my darkness, I
need you now.

THE WASP-WOMAN

after Ponge

I

She could only mate in the air. Her body,
   a little heavier than
a mosquito's, the wings light and small, beating,

hovered in a million cells. Each spent moment
   she seemed to quiver as if
pinned on a fly-paper or drowning in thick

honey. She moved as if trapped always at a
   point of crisis which made her
the danger she was. Like a taut string whose touch

burned or cut as it yielded its resonance,
   she hurt as she moved. From her
belly the rich beating came. On the skin of

plums her nails moved like a machine for plucking
   something out. If her clothes rasped
on the edge of a plate, or brushed a cup where

the dregs of sugar remained, you could feel the
   dark pull of the world's honey,
straining her muscles.

II

                     The electric tram moves

on its rails. There is something deaf in repose
   and loud into gear about
it too. It breaks at the waist as she did. Is

90

shrivelled by electricity like something
    fried. And if you touched her, she
pricked. No shock, the venomous vibration from

all her pores : but her body was softer, her
    flight wilder, more unforeseen,
more dangerous than the even run of a

thing on rails.

III

            She was one of those wheeled machines
    that at certain seasons ride
from farm to farm in the country, providing

refreshment. A little pump grinding on wings.
    Nobody knowing how she
maintained her internal state of a tense poise

or constructed what she was selling. Whose whole
    activity was inside,
a thing of mystery and presumed wisdom.

A cauldron of jam, sealed from the air, and yet
    soft. And the drum in the groin
causing her to see-saw, as she rose in flight.

IV

One must always classify what is known by
    a character which endures,
and by which one could recognise it. And so

with her it is that skin. Perhaps rightly. I
    know nothing of it, I could
never swear to it. And yet with that wasp it

was not so odd to describe her wings as *like
membranes*. Not that they looked like
a dark hymen. It was for historical

reasons. The abstraction remains, trailing the
hard truths of a thing once felt.
In the coils of the living science there lies

the stretched, gauzy, tendentious, appropriate
word for a wasp-woman. There
is nothing more in this line.

V

What else can one

say ? That she left her sting in the victim and
succumbs to it ? In war that
never pays. The elaborate touchiness —

from fear or from over-sensitivity —
has already punished her.
She has no advantage in risking a new

enemy, would zig-zag to miss a friend. *I
know my ways*, she would say, *if
I attach myself it can only provoke

a crisis. We are too far apart. If once
I accepted the pulse of
your world, I should spend my life in it. So launch

me in my groove and go on in yours. In the
sleep-walking, the internal
deadness. Forget about explaining things.* It

was then that the world gave her a little knock,
and she dropped. I could only
crush her to death.

92

VI

(Or was it perhaps that she

was touchy because of what she carried ? And
this justified her rage : her
consciousness of its value ?)

VII

And yet this fine

deadness which could destroy her (one blow, and she
dropped) could also save her, or
at least prolong her life. That dark wasp was so

stupid (I don't mean to abuse her) that if
you cut her in two parts, she
continued to live. She took two days to know

she was dead. Her heart just went on beating. It
beat faster than before. And
surely this was the zenith of preventive

stupidity ? Stupidity in the gut.

VIII

Swarm : from exagmen : from *ex
agire:* to push out.

IX

Such thirst perhaps from

the slenderness of her waist. For the Greeks the
brain was in the waist. And they
used the same word for both. If it was *sponge*, they

were right.

X

Why was it so ? That of all creatures
the fiercest one was the sun's
colour ? And why are beaten things always the

savagest ?

XI

She thrust into flesh as others
delve into fruit. Would wrestle,
mouth, warp, corrupt it. With her elastic-smooth,

marmalade-black body would smash, pulp, erase
the integrity of flesh,
even alter its feel of being alive.

When a wasp bites at a fruit there is never
such love-loathing, such many-
legged, insectuous writhing. She worked like a

black chemical, a violent process of
decomposition, marring
the flesh to a mess of pulp, exhausting the

seed.

XII

Listen to the plum speaking. *When the sun
ejaculates his honey,
it scorches my skin. If the brisk wasp works her*

sting into me, it rips my guts.

XIII

And she was
always eager for the full
honey-bin. Her temples quivering, her skin

trembling, and then the butterflies in her crutch :
   a sort of squirt for sucking
sweetness in.

XIV

      First there was the furnace. And then

the half-charred wasp was born, hissing, terrible
   and by no means a matter
of indifference to Men-kind, for they faced

in her burning elegance their abortive
   hunger for speed and for closed
flight through air. And in mine I saw an earthed fire

whose wings gushed out in all directions, and on
   unforeseen trajectories.
It burned as if on offensive missions from

a nest in the ground. Like an engine out of
   control, sometimes it trembled
as though she were not the mistress of her own

destructiveness. So at first that fire spread in
   the earth, crackling, fluttering :
and then when the wings were accomplished, the sexed

wings, the antennaed squadrons broke out on their
   deadly business into the
flesh, and their work began to be finished, I

mean, her crime.

XV

      In her swarm of words, the abrupt
waspishness. But wait. Was this
devised flutter in the trench any more than

the weak rebellion of a few seeds, outraged
    by their sower ? It was their
own violence that first brought them into his

apron. No, go back. This was a fire whose wings
    gushed out in all directions,
and on unforeseen trajectories. And I

faced in her burned elegance my abortive
    hunger for speed and for closed
flight through air. Or must one look further. Here was

the natural world on the wing. Her cruel
    divisions preparing their
offensive against male tyranny. I bared

my forests for their sting. But already her
    banked animosity was
flowing away in random fury. . . .

XVI

A swarm

of mute wasps worked over the countryside : and
    my unprotected nerves were
worked over by her.

XVII

And then one knock, one sharp

gun-shot. And she seemed (herself like a gun-shot
    recovering her fallen
decisiveness) to hurl herself with all haste

on her certain death. No, not quite. Like a shot,
    but less direct. As if when
the bullets left the gun the air seduced them

into forgetting their first intention, their
   straight road, their bitterness. Or
as if an army were sent to occupy

the nerve centres of a key city, and, once
   inside the main gates, became
absorbed into the bright things in windows, and

visited the museums, and drank from the
   straws of the men sipping wine
at the sidewalk cafés.

XVIII

         And like gun-shots the

little nibbling bites she had once taken out
   of a thing saved up : as a
wasp riddles an upright wall of wormeaten

wood.

XIX

      Or you could call her the instrument of
   that world-honey I spoke of
earlier. I mean a pent sweetness, needling,

repeated, beginning feebly, but awkward
   to shake off, and then striking
clear, with alternating force and weakness, and

so on. As the crisp wasp might well be called the
   musical form of honey :
ringing, insistent, devouring and fragile.

XX

And so on. Perhaps one day there will be a
   critic. And he will REPROACH
me for so inserting into poetry

my importunate, irritating and dead
   wasp-woman. And will DENOUNCE
the seductive appeal of her, and the way

she appears in so many sharp pieces, and
   zig-zags. And will be DISTURBED
at her lack of smooth co-ordination, and

piquancy without depth (though not without some
   danger) and all that. And will
treat my wasp-woman with all the abuse and

puzzlement she so richly deserves. I shall
   not worry, dear reader. The
harm was first done by a French poet in prose.

A LIGHT IN WINTER

I

   She sat, legs gripping, eyes
Upturning, in the front row.
      As he spoke,
Reeling through Vitruvius, she was vague
And nagging in his back mind.
       Then she asked
Something, out-urging slurred words.
         Sharp
In their intending, he took in high boots,
Voice, twisted fingers.
      As he answered, she
Hooked like an anchor, dragging at his groin
And brain.
   It ended, and the audience clashed
Towards winter traffic.
      As they broke the street,
Rain-lashed, with black cars shining, she
Hunched in her cords, mauve, belted.
       Her wet hair
Framed the bark eyes, distended, shawled
In the mist of drug-light.
     As wrecked wood, she dredged
Through tangling weeds, dense people.
       He caught up,
Switched to her step, spoke to her sidelong face
Against the crowd.
    Impulsive, as she watched him, he
Took her arm, urged her through a glass door, leaned
With her at a bar.
    Used to nothing, she
Tested his knuckles, gripped at them, drank gin
Through smoke and darkness, dodging questions.
        In

The taxi later, tongued in leather, lipped
As they rounded Hyde Park Corner, her
High legs eased, fingers opened.
                              As they rode
Against each other's bodies, briefly, he
Sensed her powered absence.
                              When she slouched out, near
Where she was living, with her number in
His calf-skin book, he waved, once.
                              She strudged in,
Clenched in her coat, stiff, man-like.
                              When he wrote
Arranging meetings, she was ill
And couldn't see him.
                              When she wrote back, he
Watched the blue, sick strokes wrangle on the page,
Sexed, wild.
                              As the need to see her fixed him tighter, he
Forgot his wife, job, only saw hard lust
Forged in a pouch for spending.
                              As he sketched
Through polished silence, or ate breakfast, poised
In jangling talk, he trembled.
                              In his bed,
Beside the jewel of his calm, his wife,
He felt an absorbed wilting.
                              So she came,
Flown from her darkness to his light.

II

                              At the place
Agreed, and in the time, oblivious to
His laid work, he sat waiting.
                              In his mind
The tower he was building dwindled.
                              When she knocked
Clutching a doll, in dark shades, barefoot, he
Shocked his firm nerves to ready taking.

100

                                    By
The steel green cases, chilled, in half-dimmed space,
They kissed, holding.
                      In soft abandon, wrapped
Over a tautness of luxurious doubt,
Her mind enriched him.
                      So they came, hands held,
To a glowing room.
                      Men bowing, instruments
Of a bored thunder, lightened.
                      By the sheets
Of traced façades, pinned elevations, tricks
And fancies of irrelevant ornament, some
Shimmered in glass, charmed, winsome.
                                    Their
Willowy consorts, offered mistresses,
Pawed, shouldered, flouncing.
                      He
Faced them, detached, observed her.
                              When she stood,
Silent, in others talking, her feet splayed,
Strange, goose-like.
                      In their eating, tumbling prawns
With a barbed fork, hot feeling found
Its symptoms.
                      They came out soon, cooled, and walked
To where she lived, hired attic.
                              In bare lust
His teeth rattled, as a skull's.
                              Her shift slid up
And over null bones, shielded.
                              Muscular
And flexing, on that sewn quilt, she
Opened her purse of illness.
                              As bent legs
Vaulted, spare arches into darkness, she
Enfranchised him in all she felt.
                              So soothed
Into her world of subtle blurring, he

                                          101

Straddled, half-dreaming.
                        Where her curved ways led
Him on, he walked in vigilant watching, ranged
Over her hills, through forests, by a stream
To the high castle.
                        In those crumbled foreign walls,
Echoing with bats and strange horns, he
Reached the jarl's table.
                        There he sat and ate,
Lifting the encrusted cup.
                        And in his dream,
Swirled in an aura of sweet scents, he dived
Into a dream of dreams.
                        Lazily, whales
And sharks moved, reeling through green weeds,
Falling and killing.
                        When he woke, or lost both, they
Gasped in a sweat of cold, wind hissing in
Through an open window.
                        It was all
It never was.

III

                        Low strangeness hung
Over his thoughts for long days.
                        She
Was in him, of him.
                        Under her thick spell
The arts of Christmas withered.
                        Her gloss card
With a black smile, some negro, and her news
Of quarrels, mess, bored ailments, filled
His days with clear light.
                        In exchange, his grooved
Whirling disc drove her furies back.
                        For hours
One night, that organ music ripped slick wings
To shreds.

102

She moved in coolness to a cave
Where someone waited.
Slow and cold,
Again those wings flicked.
He was too far in
His own concerns to care, though.
What she had
Was all the need of months for fullness, life
In the same room, a man's laugh.
He could help
Only a little, less than he knew.
So she
Planned a disaster, helpless.
In the quick
Under the covers, even as they humped
Like spoons, in close liaison, it all soured
To a head.
One night she never came
At the known time.
Then later, they
Rang in the gross night.
She was back
With slit wrists in a locked room.

IV

As he read
The brutal card that told him, bolted in
A men's-room cubicle, crude scalding drops
Melted the burned ink.
In his eyes
Her passion misted, emptied.
In dour grief
He folded what she sent, signed flowing letters, then
Graved them in memory, flushed them.
As he sat
Again beside that high glass, turning lead
In his poised fingers, he could see her arms,
Gashed, scarred.

In the watched room,
She crouched against the wall.
On a mattress, rigid
In locked fear, she spent hours.
The words rose back
Out of the blue square, swollen, blurred,
Thrashing his calm.
Day after day
Caged in that lift, as in his own taut mind,
He rose up, tried to see her.
She was tired
And seeing no-one.
In four weeks she wrote once
In sprawled mauve, Japanese felt-pen.
Illegible signs,
Frail, spidery.
He read them, wrote back, hauled
Into a pitiable chaos of longing.
Gorged
On dreams of flesh and spending, he
Showed his remoteness.
In drab hints
Noted, and swallowed, his wife grasped, and hoped,
Still, it was office trouble.
On the screen
Others played out their drama.
Here it swayed
As a slow weight.
In thin poise, to and fro,
Their union clicked and held,
Saturate with the oils of mercy.
If
Her mind risked thinking he was faithless, she
Jibbed at the huge truth.
Soon
Their bodies would resume.
And so the year
Edged to the raw Spring.

V

There, one iron day
She came out.
              In the woods and galleries
He watched her grow back.
                        With her blooded arms
Under his own, he reached for softer passion, touched
Her delicate centre.
                  Where before, their minds
Fused in a drenched rush, now
They scorched in milder fire.
                          At Putney once
They strolled in prickling sunlight, spitting pips
Of grapes in the river.
                     Tanned by inward light,
Her pitted face, pinched by the winter heat,
Faltered in smiling, as they paused.
                                  By an oak,
Racked into hollow fretwork, she stretched up
And kissed his neck.
                  He touched her razored arms,
Grown to the tree's heart.
                        So their pact was sealed
In hungry April.
              How the sadder change occurred,
And moved the cured lust from the tender love
Into excess of dullth, he never knew,
Or faced.
        For her perhaps the nub
Of change was in the stars, or in her blood,
Still blending, as do oils.
                        However it
Happened, it did so.
                  As the year burned, all
Settled, as on an isled sea.
                          Stretching to
Some edge of merging, their horizon calm
Of easy loving fooled both.

If she fretted, he
Bathed in a sweet lagoon of touching, gulfed
In swathing lust.
She grew remote, unpurged,
Ill at ease.
Each night, when he rose, dressed
And left her in the low hours, edged with fear,
She felt resentment.
That first need
For someone sane receded.
In her healed
Half-grown new mind, a drive came for a friend
Less normal, wilder.
What she needed now
Was someone like herself.
Some final test
Of mended fibre.
So the other, when he came
In burned late August, was
Inevitable, a laboratory.

VI

They had both
Gone to a stadium.
In her sheen of PVC
And plastic visor, she was modern, hip
And cured.
As an attractive decoy, she
Lolled with her legs up.
Hinting boredom, by
Her shaken hair, she caught eyes.
Under the dome
In hectic arc-light, they engaged.
White cars
Raced in the stench of violent action, wrenched
Round and round a firm track.
He sat
Locking cold numbers on a board.

106

                                        As each
Ripped and performed, he clocked them.
                                    A man leaned
In easy leather, awkward, shy,
Offering her a cigarette.
                        In the glare
Of all those egos, flowered silk and sound,
He was relaxed.
                    She talked
Into his ear, laughed, strained with words
On the board.
                    For Christ's sake take me home
And screw me, man.
                            He stayed with numbers, times,
Not caring.
                        So the paired scales hitched and slid,
Upsetting them.
                            As iron, she withdrew,
Freed from the lodestone.
                                As he went to wash,
Leaving his metal case with her, she clutched
His arm, pleaded, said not now.
                                So he went
And came back with her gone.
                                So many times
In later weeks he was to feel the same,
This jealous bile, frustrated anger, hate
For a man's hair.
                        That first night, shivering,
He drove home.
                        In the bedroom, in the dark,
Undressing softly, he heard his wife breathe
In uneasy sleep.
                        Not noticing, deaf
In his pain, he crept in, tried to join her.
                                    Crushed
In still hate, he sank under.
                                Turning, he splayed flat
On his belly, slewing rucked sheets.

                         In the heat,
Squalid with rumpled, anxious dreams, he heard
Rain, ramming the roof.
                     Outside, thin birds
With breaking feathers, lifted, hurled
Oceans of muscle into bald air.
                     As it burst
Through violence of pent wind, each was culled
Into a winnowing of silence.
                     Furrowed earth
Eased with its worms.
                     Black slugs lurched under leaves
Rustling huge drops off.
                     As he lay, he felt
Raw tension settle into troubled shaking, pin
Stiff nerve-ends.
                     Quivering, stilled,
He urged hot lips against the head-board.
                     His wife turned
Out of some dream, half-crying, rising, lapsed
Once again, as a fish would, swept
In the down-draught, to the bottom.
                     Then he slept,
Not meaning to, but tired.
                     And the storm rolled
All night.

VII

               In the morning, he rose, drove
To the tower site, over wet roads.
                     When he rang,
She sounded strange, numb.
                   In the glass box
Over his papers, he was trembling, taut
As he fixed a meeting.
                 Under the crane,
Watching the rubble swung, he saw her face
Teeming with dark fish, all day.

Tense, at eight,
He collected her, raced through the savage park
To a lonely place.
Against the wheel,
Pressing his head, he rested.
With her knees
Locked back, hair swung off, hands clawed, she
Groped in her pain to help him.
As the cars
Rocked past in flooding summer, singed with
 leaves
Out of the failing light, he saw the hands
Grip in the clock, stir, threaten.
As the sour
Injustice hit him, he heaved up, surged, struck
Her bare face, forced his whickering hand
Against her clasped legs.
In the untidy riot of clutched
Struggle in awkward space, clenched, hurt
And screaming, they scracked over chromium, glass,
Wood, stewed
In a hash of envious violence.
Then half-spilled
Through stupid angles, postures of abused
Self-hatred, they felt sex lift, steal
Into the crannies of cramped anger.
Leaning, strained
Over the leatherette arm-rest, they bunched up
In one seat, forged a broached umbrella, crammed
Each other.
When the tumbled rush had passed
In white flights to the far horizon, they
Broke into two, lay over.
All
Mended for moments, it was closeness in
Their globe.
His pride secured, he rode
Into the pleasure of remembered hope,
Forgave, and laughed.

                              She kissed him, and the stars
Crept into fresh positions, crouched for war
And evacuation.
                    They drove back
In each other's arms, knowing the falls was near
And would overwhelm them.
                              That was the last night
They even touched.

VIII

                    Far away, calm at home
In a mews yard in Hampstead, hard
In grease-pocked overalls, the blond boy worked
Racing in neutral.
                         Beside his door, high gloss
Shone on a bared, smear engine, moving parts
With inexorable power.
                              His oil-stained hands,
Uneven ways, washed straw hair, drew
Her into promises, cracked vows.
                                   As he
Sketched late, at the point block, waiting, she
Never arrived, though swearing to.
                                   One time
He took it, smiled.
                    The next, he felt hate stir
And thin despair flick.
                         So the autumn drained
Into a vacuum of envy, knowing love
Grate in its last few grains.
                              One evening, working late
Under the painful strip-lights, he
Dreamed in a waking terror.
                              He had gone
To see her, found them both there.
                                   They were lax
After love-making.

    110

When he came in, they
Woke, and then giggled, flaunting their bare skin,
Erect and goose-fleshed in his hampered face,
Famished with jealousy.

So he would seize
And work with scissors, hacking at their forks
With accurate hands.

Watch blood spurt, laughter split
Into a tattered agony of pleading.

Stop,
For God's sake, stop.

Then he found his calipers
Driven by white knuckles deep into the board,
And his arm shaking.

He unclenched his fist,
Striving to soothe himself.

IX

And then,
With no perceptible crisis, while
The chestnut walls burst open, and green mines
Exploded mahogany on gravel, he
Felt a control come.

Gradually at first,
Then tauter, with a sense of joy in things,
Love swivelled.

In his panelled house,
Dulled with the sound of ghostly breathing, all
The brooches pricked and held still.

He was lulled
Through grown content, rich pleasures.

As enwombed,
He lolled in safety, fed and sure.

His wife,
Salt in a hunger of envenoming tears,
Gathered, using her precious gains.

As she served
Him toast in a silver dish, hot soup, and kidneys, he

Grew to the will to love her.
                              Once again,
He saw the clean grace in her nose-line, sweep
Of corn-grey hair, and clean clothes.
                                   As she bent
To lift a fallen paper, pain
At so much deceit of such a sure friend sucked
Hot sobs in his throat.
                        He remembered how,
Years back, another veering ended.
                                    In
The flare of trombones it began, with fears
Of marriage breaking, then
A drying started.
                   How, he never knew,
Or couldn't think now, only that it did,
And spread until they parted.
                              After weeks,
They nudged once, in a fruit-shop.
                                   Meeting her
Over those balls, Corbusier ovals, shapes
And odours of ground, sumptuous plenty, he
Dried like a thrown pip.
                         If love winced in then,
It could now.
               And this woman, with
The dove's hair, bird of passage, tamed and swollen,
   could
Be where it aimed.
                    As he watched her body sway
In sinuous elegance, a buried lust
Shivered, he touched her.
                          Tangled in their bed,
Under the skeins of tension, wet and sleek
In oils of passion, they could swim,
Each thought, in brine of pity.
                                So,
As always, in the need to last, alive
In friendship, each accepted what there was,

112

And used it honestly.
                              He turned, and waved
In his mind, to the past.
                              In the office, when,
Days later, truth rang, he was filing.
                                        As
He set the bakelite back in
Its holder, he reflected how it seemed
So small, all bad news.
                         They
Had flown to France.
                         And so it ended, in
One sentence.
                 Why it had to, and why then,
He never knew, though knowing.

X

                         Looking out, through
That high glass, lashed with chill sleet, he
Slipped into winter, losing her.
                              Now she
Was all one with the shed seeds, fallen in
Some drift of snow.
                         Drumming the black shell
In its cradle, he began to sketch, eyes blind
With final hail, against the pain-storm.
                                        Fined
Into a second of thin terror, he
Severed it all in flared lines, flowing shapes.
Showing her, what she was.
                              Was there so much
He never knew, in madness ?
                              Now,
Under the axe, it seemed so.
                                 As he sketched
Blindly, the tower of a stone church, high
On a precipice, overlooking a long drop,
He saw her coming.

As a black, slight figure, dots
Only, in one far corner, she
Mounted a path towards the light.
A cross
Blazed, with a slung fish on the steeple, Christ
In seaward glory.
To that reach of salt and calm,
Lifting a black weight out of nowhere, she
Drove like a lost ship.
Fighting, dying now,
Into a fluxion of tense water, calmed
And still, Narcissus, she was gone.
Then the door
Opened, and his wife entered.
He tore off
The whole sheet, ripped it hard across,
Crunched it in the waste-bin.
He was back
In the plain present.
Once again
The ram broke, and across the window sleet
Swept as before, draining the light.
He rose
And took his brief-case, and went home with her,
In a dream of children, running to kiss his hands.

III

A CHILD'S GARDEN

Who was here. Before his cat
Washed and rose. Without his shoes
Who inched outside while someone's hat
Made a noise. Light feet helped. Who's.

Whose are these eggs? Ladybird's.
Hard like crumbs of sleep. She flies
Off to help who find some words
For sounds and things. Who's two puffed eyes

Tug at flowers now for bees
Tucked away. Some try to hide
In pouting fox-gloves' jugs. Who sees
Their fat bear's thighs, though, wedged inside

Scouring honey. Look ! Rare stones
In lupin leaves. Who's flapping gown
Shakes them all out. Ow ! Who's bones
Aren't awake, make who fall down

Biting earth. Who hears a sound.
Whose are these wet softish hairs
Brushing someone's mouth ? Can bound
As quick as you. Whoosh ! Peter scares

A thin bird. Zip ! Squawk ! Its beak
Almost nipped who's fattest worm
Head and tail. Who hears him squeak
Through the grass : who sees him squirm

Down a hole. Who wants to kiss
His frightened worm. Who's coolish knees
Push him up to clematis
He thinks it's called. It makes him sneeze.

Gooseflesh comes. Who's bare toes rake
Up oily slugs. Who wants to hop,
Skip. Who's flopping tassels make
Ants run. Who hears his crispies pop.

HOUSE FOR A CHILD

In a corkscrew house you start at the bottom :
You have to : and work up : it might
    Be a world, or a zoo.

Fish freeze on the blotched walls
In the steamy bathroom. I wash my knees
    With a soap poodle who

Smells clean. My thirsty elephant
Floats at my ear : I scrub my feet
    With a bristly pig.

I wrap my crumpled skin in my gown
With wiry tassels and sip juice.
    From a stool in the kitchen

The Peter plunges. He brushes my calves
With his flat sides : his tail shapes
    Ideas he has

In the air. He tortures birds when he can :
Curls in the Beanstalk : shines at night
    Like green slides

In the black garden. I tiptoe in slippers
With loud soles. I trip by the dining-room,
    Kneel and crunch

On crumbs the copper tortoise is crumbling.
I bang on his head : his back clangs up
    And I spit in him.

I nod on my heels to a spider : a quick-stepping
Elderly beetle six-foots himself over
    The blue fur

Of the close floor. I spiral up
Like a fly in a draught. From a cupboard under
       The groaning stairs

The crates creak. I bounce to the drawing-room's
Block of warmth. In a fog of heat
       I tickle the rug

With cool toes. It sheds hair
On mossy suits : laps cream paint
       With a rope tongue.

I light the shelves. The pot pigs blink.
One has a pimply back : he stares :
       If I shook him up,

Now I stare at him, I could hear him juggle
A pea in his throat. In the hall the Kodiak
       Bear by the stove

Stretches and snores. I creep on my tummy
To lie on his back : his coat's warm :
       They thwack his hide

With a hard brush to make him clean.
Good-night, Kodiak bear, sleep tight,
       I roar in his ear as

I flea him of crumbs. I shed the lights
And lock the doors. Now I jump to the bedroom
       To see my owl

Who makes me laugh : I kiss my bear
With his bashed face who keeps me safe
       And who gave his squeak

To a tiny rhino : I kick my slippers
Under the bed. I snuggle down
       Beside my pig.

When you get to the top, you have to stop
In a twiny house : unless you're a worm :
     And go to sleep.

You have to stop : unless you're a worm,
Or a bird : and say good-night : good-night :
     Good-night, world.

BEDTIME STORY

Long long ago when the world was a wild place
Planted with bushes and peopled by apes, our
Mission Brigade was at work in the jungle.
    Hard by the Congo

Once, when a foraging detail was active
Scouting for green-fly, it came on a grey man, the
Last living man, in the branch of a baobab
    Stalking a monkey.

Earlier men had disposed of, for pleasure,
Creatures whose names we scarcely remember—
Zebra, rhinoceros, elephants, wart-hog,
    Lion, rats, deer. But

After the wars had extinguished the cities
Only the wild ones were left, half-naked
Near the Equator : and here was the last one,
    Starved for a monkey.

By then the Mission Brigade had encountered
Hundreds of such men : and their procedure,
History tells us, was only to feed them :
    Find them and feed them ;

Those were the orders. And this was the last one.
Nobody knew that he was, but he was. Mud
Caked on his flat grey flanks. He was crouched, half-
    armed with a shaved spear

Glinting beneath broad leaves. When their jaws cut
Swathes through the bark and he saw fine teeth shine,
Round eyes roll round and forked arms waver
    Huge as the rough trunks

Over his head, he was frightened. Our workers
Marched through the Congo before he was born, but
This was the first time perhaps that he'd seen one.
        Staring in hot still

Silence, he crouched there : then jumped. With a long
            swing
Down from his branch, he had angled his spear too
Quickly, before they could hold him, and hurled it
        Hard at the soldier

Leading the detail. How could he know Queen's
Orders were only to help him ? The soldier
Winced when the tipped spear pricked him. Unsheathing
            his
        Sting was a reflex.

Later the Queen was informed. There were no more
Men. An impetuous soldier had killed off,
Purely by chance, the penultimate primate.
        When she was certain,

Squadrons of workers were fanned through the Congo
Detailed to bring back the man's picked bones to be
Sealed in the archives in amber. I'm quite sure
        Nobody found them

After the most industrious search, though.
Where had the bones gone ? Over the earth, dear,
Ground by the teeth of the termites, blown by the
        Wind, like the dodo's.

WHEN I AM DEAD

I desire that my body be
properly clothed. In such things
as I may like at the time.

And in the pockets may there be
placed such things as I use at the time
as pen, camera, wallet, file.

And I desire to be laid on my side
face down : since I have bad dreams
if I lie on my back.

No one shall see my face when I die.

And beside me shall lie
my stone pig
with holes in his eyes.

And the coffin shall be as big as a crate.
No thin box
for the bones only.

Let there be room for a rat to come in.

And see that my cat, if I have one then,
shall have my liver.
He will like that.

And lay in food for
a week and a day :
chocolate, meat, beans, cheese.

And let all lie in
the wind and the rain.
And on the eighth day burn.

And the ash
scatter as the wind decides.
And the stone and metal be dug in the ground.

This is my will.

OWL

is my favourite. Who flies
like a nothing through the night,
who-whoing. Is a feather
duster in leafy corners ring-a-rosy-ing
boles of mice. Twice

you hear him call. Who
is he looking for ? You hear
him hoovering over the floor
of the wood. O would you be gold
rings in the driving skull

if you could ? Hooded and
vulnerable by the winter suns
owl looks. Is the grain of bark
in the dark. Round beaks are at
work in the pellety nest,

resting. Owl is an eye
in the barn. For a hole
in the trunk owl's blood
is to blame. Black talons in the
petrified fur ! Cold walnut hands

on the case of the brain ! In the reign
of the chicken owl comes like
a god. Is a goad in
the rain to the pink eyes,
dripping. For a meal in the day

flew, killed, on the moor. Six
mouths are the seed of his
arc in the season. Torn meat
from the sky. Owl lives
by the claws of his brain. On the branch

in the sever of the hand's
twigs owl is a backward look.
Flown wind in the skin. Fine
rain in the bones. Owl breaks
like the day. Am an owl, am an owl.

NOAH'S JOURNEY

I

The Building of The Ark

oak

is the keel. He is agèd and
gnarl-faced. See, he is here
with his acorns and edged leaves.
Off with his bark and his big
roots. Oak is an old friend.
Lays down his light beams, dips
them in warm tar : submits to
a varnish on one side. Is all
washed and ready for when storm comes.

I am well-grained. I lie flat,
hold off the water and float on
the waves. Once grounded, I
wait for a sailing, alert in the sun.

pine

is the mast. He is upright,
smooth, straight and long-limbed.
He moves like a ramrod,
casting aside all his twigs and his
branches. A few cones
curling an eyebrow predict when the
rain's due. Standing in place now,
spun in a socket he sets like a
maypole. An oiled bole of red wood.

Screwed to the low deck, I
rise to the cold stars. The sea waits,
tossing a little. The black earth
lingers to wave me a long farewell.

The Entry of the Animals

mouse

> comes first. You can find
> him in holes. Out of the steel
> trap he would take your cheese
> with a flip of his foot. But, phlung !
> down the hard cold hat comes and
> is off with his ears. Is it
> so, mouse ? Out of your wooden
> house come, mouse, and answer me.
> There is work for your teeth in the ark.

> > *Noah, Noah, I dare not come*
> > *out. There are too many cats.*
> > *And I fear for my tail. I will*
> > *come for some Brie.*

bat

> flies next like a broken
> umbrella. Are you there, blind
> bat, in the wind and the dark ?
> You may squeak in the hold to
> the spider in the beam. I will
> mend your wing. There are sound-
> proofed boards for your sensitive
> ears. Come down, sharp bat, with
> your wife, and be friends.

> > *I am here all the time at*
> > *your hand. So quietly I flew*
> > *that you never knew. I am*
> > *warm in the pit of your arm, blind Noah.*

rat

leaves a sinking ship. Wise
brown rat, is there blame in that?
If you have to leave the
ark you must oar your way out
with an ant and a ladybird
aloft on your snout. Rat, make a
ring, be a life-belt here.
And gnaw me a port-hole or two
to see through. That will keep you quiet.

Rough Noah, I will not. I prefer
a biscuit. And as for sinking,
why it doesn't bear thinking. I
will nip your ankle if you nag at me.

lynx

is my look-out. He can see
in the murk. Yellow falls the
fog but the perk-eared lynx
feels vigilant. On the branch of
the mast he is pinned by his
claws. Telescoped in muscle
waits lynx for the land. With
a leap he will land, be the
first one on Ararat. Eh, peaked lynx?

I am anxious to rest my eyes.
Keep me away from the dazzle of
the zebra and the dots of the
leopard. I will stare at the plain bear.

pig

will need guiding with this
boar board. He is heavy with
acorns. Incontinent pig!

Why did they send me a pig
so big ? You must learn to
be slimmer from the wolf or
the hare. I will fit you in
below decks. But you must keep
still, and not overlay any beast.

> *I am usefully fat. I can*
> *keep some warm. There is sure*
> *to be ice. And I shan't*
> *need heat.*

bear

are you there ? Why, you smell
of honey. You voracious small bear !
Why have you come with your paws all
sticky ? Go down to the sink.
You must dance for your
supper, and it won't be sweets.
Coarse brown bread for omnivorous
bears. And a beaker of brine
if we have to keep washing you in drinking water.

> *I am sorry, Noah. But I grew*
> *quite faint. So I stopped by a hive*
> *for a rest and a meal.*
> *Let me give you a hug.*

tiger

is a stick along railings. Like a
ripple in a lake he has lodged
in your eye. Come, tiger, you
are here. Tensed sinews in the rain.
Stretch out on the poop. Glare
over the orb of the ocean and
frighten the hail. We are safe,
mewed up in our tub with a
tiger to care for us. Tiger, look fierce.

With a roar and a bounce I
will tear up the clouds. Keep
plenty of meat, though, for me. I will
wait like a rug.

crocodile

creeps out of the swamp with a
creak and a snap. He is made like a
bag. He can float for a day
without winking his eye. In the mud
of the bayou he has pondered the flood
and decided to miss it. So come in,
long crocodile, and crawl to your space.
You can help make logs. We shall soon
need a fire. Lie there, and snap.

I would snap with a will. I have
toothache, though. Please, Noah, will you
give me a pill. In a mouth like mine
pain sprouts like a bush.

rhinoceros

comes aboard like a boulder. He is
lapped in hard layers like a
hot-water tank. We must study
him hard to improve the ark's
lagging. What a load you are
for us, lily-eared rhinoceros ! If
you were to jump we should
plump to the bottom. Stand here
on this stout plank. And have some hay.

I don't eat hay. I am
sorry, I must say, to be such
a burden. Will it help if I lift
my little ox-pecker off ?

132

elephant

comes last in his loose grey skin. In
the sun you can see brown
hairs on his back. I am sure he
will help to haul the ark
along the flat canal to the flood
when the water has come. He is
not forgetful of all the food
he will need. Have you brought green
leaves, ant-like and prudent elephant?

Aye, aye, Noah, I have hauled
this tree. It will feed huge me
for a year. Is there space
in the barge?

whale

must swim by the side of
the ship. If I take a dip
I can ride safe back on his
broad black head. Whale is
the biggest, are you not,
vast whale? In a storm you
can shelter the ship from the
waves. I will feed you for this
with plenty of plankton.

I am partial to plankton. I will
swim by your side. Yes, I will swim
by the ark's hind rim
and soothe the poor beasts who are sick.

The Battle with the Elements

thunder

is the one who is blundering
about. I can hear him in the
sky like a lout in the attic.
Bricks he would hurl if he
had them. Bing. Bang. He is
round like a gong with a
big bronze face. Say boo to
a goose he would not were it
not for his flick-nosed cousin.

*Talk big, small man, while you
can. I will bash you. Just
give me a minute to blow up
my balloon. You wait.*

lightning

is another. O another
matter. Snears through the ether
like a spear. Shrip-shrivels
into shreds your elaborate
ladders. Is a daze on the
deck. Stiff blitz to the sheets.
Fit scissors for the ropes
of the bark's tossed body. In a fit
you are cracked, split, ruined.

*Nix, Noah, you exaggerate a
little. You're afloat. I can
see a green pug-dog awash in the stern,
but the fireworks are finished, I'm off to bed.*

rain

is the one who goes on. He is flung
pita-pata-pita-pata from a
tipped bowl of dry peas. Wet fur,
wet wood, wet wings, wet canvas : the
whole wide world is awash in a
sluice of beans. Rattle, rush.
Down comes the roof in a slush
of cold glass bits. Below decks
glum beasts peer out and steam dry slowly.

I pour on. Always in
motion, a flow in the air, I
slither to all points. And fill earth
top-full of water, of water, of water.

wind

is the last one. A wild thing,
over the flat sea, the smooth
sea, he wanders. Whistling a
thin tune, a high tune, a shrill tune,
whirling the waves to a white, whizzed,
whipped-cream. Zing, zing, zing : and the
ark like a roundabout rolls up and
down, up and down, in a frenzy.
Packed close like sardines, the poor beasts are
all sick.

I breathe on. Puffing my fat
cheeks, I fill the small ship's
sails: blow it towards sand,
send it to new shores.

grass

grows beyond rock. The fur
of the soaked earth. The sweet
green coat of the land we
must stand upon. Ho, there, grass.
Are you dry behind the ears after all
that rain ? Are you ready
for my green-fly to clamber in
your hair ? Make room for
my elephant to land on your hide.

Noah, you may safely land. I was the
first to dry. This is your
warm and expected haven. And
here is your long-lost dove and your raven.

THE RED HERRING

after Cros

There was once a high wall, a bare wall. And
against this wall, there was a ladder,
a long ladder. And on the ground,
under the ladder, there was a red
herring. A dry red herring.

And then a man came along. And in his hands
(they were dirty hands) this man had
a heavy hammer, a long nail
(it was also a sharp nail) and
a ball of string. A thick ball of string.

All right. So the man climbed up
the ladder (right up to the top)
and knocked in the sharp nail :
spluk ! Just like that.
Right on top of the wall. The bare wall.

Then he dropped the hammer. It dropped
right down to the ground. And onto the nail
he tied a piece of string, a long
piece of string, and onto the string
he tied the red herring. The dry red herring.

And let it drop. And then he climbed
down the ladder (right down
to the bottom), picked up the hammer
and also the ladder (which was pretty heavy)
and went off. A long way off.

And since then, that red herring, the dry
red herring on the end of the string, which is
quite a long piece, has been
very very slowly swinging and
swinging to a stop. A full stop.

I expect you wonder why I made
up this story, such a simple story. Well,
I did it just to annoy people.
Serious people. And perhaps also
to amuse children. Small children.

MARSHALL

It occurred to Marshall
that if he were a vegetable, he'd
be a bean. Not
one of your thin, stringy
green beans, or your

dry, marbly
Burlotti beans. No, he'd be
a broad bean,
a rich, nutritious,
meaningful bean,

alert for advantages,
inquisitive with potatoes,
mixing with every kind
and condition of vegetable,
and a good friend

to meat and lager. Yes, he'd
leap from his huge
rough pod with a loud
popping sound
into the pot : always

in hot water
and out of it with a soft
heart inside
his horny carapace. He'd
carry the whole

world's hunger on
his broad shoulders, green
with best butter
or brown with gravy. And if
some starving Indian saw his

flesh bleeding
when the gas was turned on
or the knife went in
he'd accept the homage and prayers,
and become a god, and die like a man,

which, as things were, wasn't so easy.

AT CRUFT'S

I

Old English Sheep-dog

Eyes
drowned in fur :
an affectionate,

rough, cumulus
cloud, licking
wrists and

panting : far
too hot
in your

"profuse" coat
of old wool. You
bundle yourself

about on
four shaggy
pillars

of Northumberland
lime-stone,
gathering sheep.

II

Weimaraner

On long
monkey's-paws
like

olive-branches, you
loll, awkwardly
leaning

your dun muzzle against
the veined
oak : your

eyes are what
matter most, those
bottomless, dreaming

yellows, orbed
in
the fine bone

of a German
hunter's-rifle
head.

III

Chow

With ears
of a Teddy bear : your
tail

over-curled
as if attempting
to open

yourself
like a tin
of pilchards : your tongue

seal-blue : you
roll
in a cuddly

world
of
muscular

bunches, bouncy as
Chinese
India-rubber.

IV

Shih Tzu

Top-knot
in a safety-
pin, this

grand-master,
flexible
as a rug, flops,

inclines
his grave head,
is a blur

to the Japanese
photographer,
some foreign

bitch, is he
thinking,
as he wraps

his fleece
in imaginary
sleeves.

V

Chinese Crested

Raw
as a skinned
chicken, the

goat's plume
on your brow
ruffled, you

swing a
furred
switch

in the ring
behind you,
fastidiously

tripping
more like a gazelle
than a dog

as you move :
Manchurian,
shivering.

VI

Schnautzer

In that
severe
square hook

of a head, he
holds outlines
of his own

dour
elegance to be
scissored

in air : braced
legs
erect

his arched
eyebrows : in grey
mournful

exactitude, his
jaw swivels and :
schnapps !

VII

Bulldog

With a face
as crumpled
as crushed

paper, he
shoulders
grumpily

over the sawdust :
someone pats
his

rear, he is
sure,
nevertheless, there

is still
a war on. Everything
everywhere,

pace Leibnitz,
is for
the worst.

VIII

Dobermann

Always
on the attack, the lips
drawn

hard back, the
minute
immaculate

teeth, bared
in a snarl, no
love

lost, is
there, then,
between us, or

wasted; in
smooth black
and orange

killing skin
you sit,
spring-coiled.

IX

Shetland Sheep-dog

Am I being
so thoroughly
powdered

146

to win
a prize, or
just

to please
this ingenious
powderer

in her
pink anorak, you
seem to ask,

with your bright
ice-chips
ripping

the prejudice from
your over-
fluffy ruff.

X

Pyrenean Mountain Hound

As if
absorbing the whole
heat of snow

into his noble
coat, he
lifts,

heavy-lidded, the
sombre
gaze

of a glacier-
liver,
knowing

not only how
to revive
the frozen

with brandy, but
what
being wanted means.

XI

Newfoundland

Is
a black
solid-bodied

one this, with
a look
of lying

beside a
banked fire,
stretched

in his log-
cabin, his nose
twitching

to the sound
of owls or
coyotes, or even

coal
dropping
in the grate.

XII

Clumber Spaniel

If ears
are for hearing
with,

she seems to
waste
acres of expensive

velvet, her
brindled
flaps relaxing

in
friendly
fingers, although,

quite definitely,
closed : at any rate, she
goes

on
dozing
without saying a word.

XIII

Great Dane

To be so
big
you could

easily
over-leap my
six feet with your

coat of
many
colours, fawn,

black, harlequin,
is,
after all,

remarkable
enough, so
why whip

my legs
to a jelly
with your tail?

XIV

Boston Terrier

Neat
enough for
a tea-party

in that flat
alpaca coat, you
maintain, though, something of

a lawyer's look,
my mid-Victorian,
Yankee

dandy, round-
supercilious-
eyed, fresh

from the courts
after quartering
someone, perched

on your four
ebony
sticks.

XV

Samoyed

As if
presenting the
spun glitter of

a new
steel wool : or an
ice tasting

of glacier-
mint : this
polar bundle of

huggable
whiteness, clear
hair

emerging
like tufts
of grown

glass from her
deep skin,
glows.

XVI

Alsatian

And yet
without exactly the
appearance of

being violent,
that heavy
tail, tucked

under the firm
hind-quarters,
occasions

doubts about the
advisability
of treating

this law-dog
as if
he was really only

a sheep
in wolf's-
clothing.

XVII

Irish Setter

Touch the flowing
thorough-bred
insouciance

of the Old
Ascendancy : the
superior-tweed

mahogany
fur, glossy
as if wet

from the best kind
of trout-stream
recently,

ruffles, furrows
a little
over

the interrogating,
courteous arrogance
of the eyes.

XVIII

Boxer

On a strong
rope,
aggressive,

restrained, you
tug
at your corner,

eager
for the bell, and
to be in,

dancing
round the ring,
belligerent in

your
gloved skin,
muscled

as if to
let fists
emerge, clenched.

FOURTEEN WAYS
OF TOUCHING THE PETER

I

You can push
your thumb
in the
ridge
between his
shoulder-blades
to please him.

II

Starting
at its root,
you can let
his whole
tail
flow
through your hand.

III

Forming
a fist
you can let
him rub
his bone
skull
against it, hard.

IV

When he makes
bread,
you can lift
him
by his under-
sides on your
knuckles.

V

In hot
weather
you can itch
the fur
under
his chin. He
likes that.

VI

At night
you can hoist
him
out of his bean-stalk,
sleepily
clutching
paper bags.

VII

Pressing
his head against
your cheek,
you can carry
him
in the dark,
safely.

VIII

In late Autumn
you can find
seeds
adhering
to his fur.
There are
plenty.

IX

You can prise
his jaws
open,
helping
any medicine
he won't
abide, go down.

X

You can touch
his
feet, only
if
he is relaxed.
He
doesn't like it.

XI

You can comb
spare thin
fur
from his coat,
so he won't
get
fur-ball.

XII

You can shake
his rigid
chicken-leg leg,
scouring his
hind-quarters
with his Vim
tongue.

XIII

Dumping
hot fish
on his plate, you can
fend
him off,
pushing
and purring.

XIV

You can have
him shrimp
along you,
breathing,
whenever
you want
to compose poems.

TO A SLOW DRUM

a stately music

I

Solitary thoughts,
and burial mounds,
begin this dirge,
and mournful sounds.

II

Now to the dead march
troop in twos,
the granite owls
with their *Who Was Who's*,
the bat, and the grave, yew
bear on his wheels,
Tuborg the pig
with his hard wood heels.

III

Gemmed with a dew
of morning tears,
the weeping armadillo
has brought his shears :
the droop-ear dog
and the lion come,
dipping their long waists
to meet the drum.

IV

On the bare chafing-dish
as each one hears,
the grey lead pigs
reverse their spears :

grooved in line,
they show no grief,
            grouped above a sere
and yellow leaf,
            a tree's life blown
through a crack in the door.

V

            Over the red-black
kitchen floor,
            Jeremy the spider
stalks to his place,
            all eight legs
wet from the waste :
            he climbed up the drain
to be here on time.

VI

            Now, to the slow
egg-timer's chime,
            shiny in state
come things from the grime :
            tiny slaters
with wings and hoods,
            beetles from the closet
under the stairs :
            gashed with sorrow
each fixed eye stares.

VII

            Fairbanks crawls
from his winter leaves :
            he rubs his eyes
on his prickling sleeves :
            rattling his plate
for a sad sound,

                his black legs cover
the chill ground
                at a fair speed :
he creeps to our need.

VIII

                Now the hall resounds
to the tread of toes
                as each one gathers,
and the crowd grows :
                broken-spirited,
the bears upstairs
                troop to the banisters
and droop their ears :
                the brown one squats,
glum cheeks in his paws,
                the blue one strums
a melancholy string.

IX

                From all feasts of fish
he wove good fur:
                alas, no fish
stale death can deter.

X

                As the drum beats,
the long cortège
                winds to the attic
as towards the stage :
                some hop and skip,
some crawl or run,
                the sad music
holds every one :

160

        crouched by the window
all weep to view
        Peter, poor Peter,
drift up the flue.

XI

        Now, all together
they chant his dirge,
        grouped by the ledge
where the chimneys merge.

XII

        Peter, salt Peter,
fish-eating cat,
        feared by the blackbird,
stung by the gnat,
        wooden-spider collector,
lean as a rat,
        soon you shall fall
to a fine grey fat.

XIII

        Peter, salt Peter,
drift into the wind,
        enter the water
where all have sinned:
        forgive us our trespasses
as we forgive yours:
        remember us in heaven
as clean scales and furs,
        as we you on earth here
when any cat purrs.

XIV

Peter, salt Peter,
farewell and live,
        as we do remembering
and so forgive.

XV

Over the whole world
a sad pall falls,
        fur into fine air,
bone into ash :
        a chill water
wets every lash.

XVI

Peter, salt Peter,
by pleurisy slain,
        the pale glass weeps
in its wooden pane,
        come to the cat-flap
and slap in again.

XVII

Peter, salt Peter,
the bird of death,
        a boding raven
chokes off my breath.

XVIII

Wrung warm tears,
and doleful words
        end this dirge,
and the screams of birds.

IV

SCISSOR-MAN

I am dangerous
    in a crisis
with sharp legs and a screw

    in my genitals. I slice
bacon-rind for a living. At nights I
    lie dried

under the draining-board, dreaming
    of Nutcrackers
and the Carrot-grater. If I should

    catch him rubbing
those tin nipples of hers
    in the bread-bin

(God rust his pivot!) so much for
    secrecy. I'd have his
washer off. And

    then what? It scarcely pays
to be 'Made In Hamburg'. Even
    our little salt-spoon

can sound snooty
    with an E.P.N.S. under
his armpit. Even the pie-server

    who needs re-dipping. In sixteen
stainless years dividing
    chippolata-links I

am still denied
    a place in the sink unit. And
you can imagine

what pairing-off is possible
with a wriggle of cork-screws
in an open knife-box. So I

keep my legs
crossed. I never cut up
rough. I lie with care

in a world where a squint leg
could be fatal. I sleep like a weapon
with a yen for a pierced ear.

A TRUE STORY

When the British Association
For the Advancement of Science held
Its Annual Meeting one year in
    East Anglia no-one could

Think what to feed them on. It appeared
From previous experience in
County Durham that members consumed
    An enormous quantity

Of sandwiches. How were the hundreds
Of visiting scientists to be
Fed ? The problem was finally solved
    By the inspiration of

A Norfolk poacher who suggested
At a public meeting in the Town
Hall at Norwich the employment of
    Their local pest the Coypu

Rat. He claimed that between two layers
Of freshly cut bread a thick slice of
Coypu tasted quite delicious. And
    It proved so. At any rate

The sandwiches were bought and eaten
In extraordinarily large
Numbers. The plain bread seemed to set off
    The unusual taste of

The dead rodent. Indeed a group of
Younger men from the Biology
Section dissected the furry beasts
    With a view to assessing

Just why. Altogether it was 'a
Great success for the quality of
Willingness to experiment' as
　　'The Countryman' aptly said.

TOYS

made in Japan

I

Myst-All

In a blown
glass
double
bubble,
sealing

a vacuum, a
few
scraps of
red metal
obstruct

the orifice of
a thin
internal
spire.
Up it,

when clutched
in a hot
executive
hand,
methyl alcohol

is sucked,
and
boils
to the
body's heat,

making
them spin,
and tinkle,
fretfully,
in the top.

II

Footballer

On a wooden
pillar, a
pink,
leaning,
American
footballer
stands.
Above his
padded head, he
holds a
wooden pole
on the ends of
which are a
pair of
painted footballs.
When you
push him, he
sways, jigs
on his poised
wooden feet, and,
however hard you
hit him, or
hit his wooden pole, or
hit the footballs on the
ends of his pole, he
never topples, or
loses his balance, but
only slowly

rocks to

weight from one

other

he regains his

with a delicate

tippety-tap, he

to a neat

and fro, tilting his

foot to the

until

balance, and then

tip-tap

dances

halt.

WHAT METRE IS

it is a matter
of counting (five
syllables in the first line, four
in the second) and

so on. Or we can change to
seven words in the first line
six in the second. Is
that arbitrary ?

Prose is another possibility. There could be three
sentences in the stanza. This would be an example of
that.

Which (on the other hand)
we could lay out
by a letter count, as (this by the way is
free verse, without metre)

'pro
se is another possib
ility. There could be th
ree sent
ences in the st
anza. This would be an exam
ple of that.' I mean
it is a matter
of mathematics. Intervals between
the words, three to
a line is the
rule here. It results

in the same as
having words, four to
a line. In the
mind of the poet,
though, it makes a
difference. White spaces
(now it is two spaces) are

just articulation,
space, words
(now it
is one)

mean
something

(now
it
is
words) and

no it is
not
music either. Internal
rhyming (though sometimes
the kernel of new ideas) is
a matter of timing.

The same is true for
rhythm, the beat
(two to a line
it is here)

only becomes like a rhythm when
as here it moves with a regular
dactyl or two to a line. If

slow now spondees
make lines move, stiff

rhythm is metre (in dactyls again) but
rhythm is usually not
like this. In a word

it can escalate
drop

do as it pleases
move freely
(look out, I'm coming)

stop
at a stop

and so on. Assonance
that semblance
(except in Owen)
a, when

it works, echo
of awkwardness is O.K.

but not for me : nor is lively
alliteration

leaping
long lean and allusive
through low lines. It

becomes a matter
of going back
to metre, ending w

ith its mos
t irrit
ating (perhaps) manif
estation thi
s inarticul

ate mechanical stu
tter. It is the voi
ce of the type-wr
iter. It is the abdic
ation of insp

iration. I li
ke it. It i
s the logica

l exp
ression o
f itsel
f.

AT THE HOUSE OF JADE

from the Chinese of Fan Chung Yen (A.D.989–1052)

'leaves drifting – cold – house empty – absence – lamp-
light – loneliness'

SL   IF
EE   T.
V

E
S   I
DR   HO

                 US
                 E
                 A

                 B
                 SE
                 NC

                 E.

                 L

                 I
                 GH
                 T

                 IN
                  L
                 O

                 N
                 EL
                 Y

CO
LD

,

LA
MP

L
EA
V

E
S
ME

L
ES
S

OL
D

LE
AV
E

S
.
E

AV
ES

E
MP
TY

```
      A
      MP
      L

      E
        L
        IE
      S.

      H

      O
        WI

      I

      KN
        OW

      I


        E
      VE

      'S
        R
      I

      F
      T
        AL

      ON
        E
      L

      I
        ES
        D
```

RI
FT
I

N
G
L

IG
HT

I
N
EM

PT
Y
C

O
LD
.

I
S
H

I
FT
H

OU
SE
,

LI
GH

T
MY

L
AM
P.

IF

S
HE
I

S
AB
S

E
NC
E,

 L
EA
V

E
S
DR

IF
T
I

N   (2–2–1
 M   1–2–2
E.   alternately)

FOR CHI-CHI

on her arrival in Moscow

'snow – airport – panda – flash-bulbs – mate'

```
S        N        O        W
L        A        S        H                E
S        .        S        D                A
I        R                 A                A
T        E        S        A                P
A        N        D                         S
.                          A
         O        R        T
P        A        T        E                S
S                 A        P                A
.N       D        O        S
N        N        S        W
K        O                 B                U
N        B        A        .
L        M        F
                  U        T                E
S                 A        L                A
S        H                 N                O
S        B        A        L                B
         D        O        P                A
S        N        U        S
N                 A        W                .
K
```

181

PAVAN FOR AN UNBORN INFANTA

AN-AN CHI-CHI
AN-AN CHI-CHI

CHI-CHI AN-AN
CHI-CHI AN-AN

CHI-AN

CHI-AN CHI-AN CHI-AN CHI-AN CHI
AN-CHI AN-CHI AN-CHI AN

CHI-AN CHI-AN CHI-AN CHI-AN CHI
AN-CHI AN-CHI AN-CHI AN

CHI-AN

AN-CHI AN-CHI AN-CHI AN
AN-CHI AN-CHI AN-CHI AN

CHI-CHI

AN-AN CHI-CHI
AN-AN CHI-CHI

CHI-CHI AN-AN
CHI-CHI AN-AN

AN-AN

AN-AN AN-AN AN-AN AN-AN

CHI-CHI CHI-CHI CHI-CHI
CHI-CHI CHI-CHI CHI-CHI

CHI-CHI

AN-AN AN-AN
AN-AN AN-AN

AN-AN AN-AN
AN-AN AN-AN

AN-AN

CHI-CHI CHI-CHI
CHI-CHI CHI-CHI

CHI-CHI CHI-CHI
CHI-CHI CHI-CHI

CHI-CHI

THE LAX CHEER

I
ro
be
rt
l
ax

r
ob
er
t
la
x;

ro
be
rt
l
ax

r
ob
er
t
la
x

ro
be
rt
l
ax

184

r
ob
er
t
la
x

II

la
x

la
x

la
x

III

r
ob
er
t

r
ob
er
t

IV

l
ax

l
ax

185

V

ro
be
rt

ro
be
rt

VI

l
ax
r
ob
er
t

la
x
ro
be
rt

l
ax
r
ob
er
t

la
x
ro
be
rt

l
ax
r
ob
er
t

la
x
ro
be
rt

THE NAPOLEON BLUES

I

ab
l
wa
si

el
b
saw
i

II

i
air
i

i
air
i

III

saw
i

wa
si

saw
i

wa
si

IV

i
air
i

i
air
i

V

ab
l
wa
si
air

el
bas
aw
i
air

VI

i
air
i

i
air
i

VII

saw
i
air

wa
si
air

VIII

i
air
i

i
air
i

IX

ab
l
wa
si
air

el
bas
aw
i
air

X

saw
i
air

wa
si
air

XI

i
air
i

i
air
i

TWO EXPERIMENTS

I

Vowel Analysis of "Babylonian Poem"

from the German of Friederike Mayröcker

"U EE-EI A I AE-IIE-EIE UE EOE U EI ; E
EI AAAU (A U EI ? OE EEUE E I O EE
    O EIE AUE (EE) ;
EUE E ; AOAIE EI)
EUIOEA ; AU EIE AUEAAE IE EE-O (EI . . .)

EO AUE : OE IE A . . ."EEE A E UE
    EI E-O ; EI A ; A UE . . ."
U AUEUE A ; EI U A ;
O-E/AU UE
EUE IEE A IEEE UE
AAI I E OOE E I

OI O UA : AUI IE AEIE : U AEE E ; OE O ;
UIE EA U EE EIEAE ; UE EAUE AE ;
    A ; EI-A-AU . . ."

AU/EIE E OI I A AE UEAIE A
IAUE A-II ;
EIE OIE A I EE (IU A E AE ; UE
    EIE AAEE OEEI I EEOIE EIE)
A-OIE ; I OEE EIE ; OAE EI EUEU ;
EA IE AE—AUA ; AAEI ; AAEI (EO
    OE-U U-I-AAE . . .)

UAUIE AO !
UAE ; IE OE-/OIEE EA-A-A ! EO
    O-EIE . . . (A EIE EIEI I E EIE U ?)

IAIIEE EI-IEE
AI AIAIEE AE ; UE ; AA ; EE
...EI AUO UE EIE-E
AUOE..."OI E A..."/A-OI OU' E E...U A-A !
EIE EAE OE-A ;
A-AU-E
AAE AIA (IE
    AOE U AOIE : OAUE ; OAI ; AO)

O-EI-O : OO-I-OU !

EA A AEI/

    (IAUUAIO E OE EEI)

II

Numerical Analysis of "Brazilian Poem"
    from the German of Friederike Mayröcker

    ("..2 2 6 2 3 5: 2 3 3–6 3 8; 3
        6 9 4 8 8; 3 6 10;
        9 3 5; 2–2: 5 4 6!
        2 10 6 6 (8) – 4 3 6 11;
        5 6; 8 7; 2 3 6..")

          9 5 3 5: 2 3 2
      10 4
5 8; 3 9 2 3; 5 3 4 3 3 9 9: (4 !)
3 6 3 3 4 – 9 6; 7
3 3 5; 8; 3 3 6; 10 (3 3 7 4 2 3 !)

9 4 3 5 6: 6 3 10:
        5 3 5 7..

4–5 4 9–6 3 5 3 8;
4 7 2 5 6 4: 7 3 3 8
       3 11 5
9 10 (7 2 6) 7 5 3 6–5:
(8 5) – 4 2 6 4: 10 5!
3 3 6 9 6
            (5 4 4)
               (5 4 5)

7 2 5;
3 11 3 4–5

6 4 3 15 4 (6 5)

! 2 6! 3 2 3 6 10 6;
! 2 6!
(10 5 5 4; 10 5 4 5)

2 6 –

       (2 1 7 2 3?)
9

LDMN ANALYSIS OF
THOMAS NASHE'S *SONG*

```
D,  LL   L,
LD NN  ,
ND   L LLL  ,
D   M LL      ,
NN M   D N L,
M  ,   M D:
     LD   M N  .


MN,  N N L,
LD NN    L,
ML M D.
LL N,   ND   MD,
L LL        ,
M  ,   M D:
     LD   M N  .


L,
NL LL D,
N LL M    ,
N   DD N, ND  ,
D   LD LN  .
M  ,    M D:
     LD   M N  .


N  N  ,
M D N    ,
D M N      ,
LL LD      .
M, M,   LL D .
M  ,   M D:
     LD   M N  .
```

NN,
D N :
L N,
N
N   N L.
M ,   M D :
     LD   M N .

D ,
LM DN :
N   ,
L ,
MN   N   .
M ,   M D :
     LD   M N .

ODE ON A GRECIAN URN

after Keats

I

You're not
more than a fresh girl
in a cool church,
                              now are
you ?
                  Cross of a few
thousand centuries, and
not much noise,
                              you
got your bland touch
with the country stuff
                                    (I grant
you, lusher than mine)
through lasting
                              simply,
frocked with tree-myths
in ghost-fashion,
                              gods
and us,
                  and a garnish
of coy girls, lechers,
rape, riot, and
                        the final
big O.

II

It's always
easier on the ear
not to have the
                        music
actually *playing*.
                        I

mean, if the oboe
tickles the fine roots
of the metaphysical
                    man, not
the material one, you
draw a bonus.
                    As,
for example, that
fine boy there
                    in the clearing, he
won't ever get
what he's after, or
                    see
(for that matter) the
leaves fall,
                    but she'll
be as Camay-fresh
and desirable
                    tomorrow, that
cool bint with
the Jimi Hendrix.

III

Once you have
the consummation, it's
your swollen eyes, your
                    morning
sickness and your Alka-
Seltzer.
                    Whereas here,
I grant you, they're
all swinging, even
the vocalist,
                    and
the trees.
                    As for
those kids, warm
in each other's

                    expectations,
aren't they just
having a ball,
                    static
in glazed love,
and with all the new tunes !

                    IV

     Take the religious
piece, too.
                    I agree
it's far better
from the cow's point
                    of view,
not to be having
that funny boy with
                    the dog-collar
really getting down
to his carve-up
                    in the grove.
So she goes on
all smooth and flowery, and
                    mooing, too.
Then there's the bare city
beside the water,
                    with the lynch-mob
all gone off to
their blood-letting,
                    and not a soul
left with a bad story
to tell the sheriff
                    about
where they are, and who with.
It helps, it
                    helps.

V

Yes, you have
us all voting
for Miss Timeless,
          the Greek
bird with the
curvy look.
       She
has it all made,
the cold-as-marble look,
          the few
twigs in her hair,
the down-trodden stance.
          When we're
all grey, and fucked up,
(and it's coming)
          you'll be there,
still charming, a mite cool
maybe, to our minds
          in our troubles
but (and here's good news)
bearing the same message :
          life's a bowl
of cherries, if you believe it,
if you believe it, life's
          a bowl of cherries. That's
the big secret, man,
the only secret.

THE CRAB-APPLE CRISIS

for Martin Bell

'To make this study concrete I have devised a ladder — a metaphorical ladder — which indicates that there are many continuous paths between a low-level crisis and an all-out war.'

'On Escalation' by Herman Kahn

Level I: Cold War

Rung 1: Ostensible Crisis

Is that you, Barnes ? Now see here, friend. From
where I am I can see your boy quite
clearly soft-shoeing along towards
my crab-apple tree. And I want you

to know I can't take that.

Rung 2: Political, Economic and Diplomatic Gestures

If you don't
wipe that smile off your face, I warn you
I shall turn up the screw of my frog
transistor above the whirr of your

lawn-mower.

Rung 3: Solemn and Formal Declarations

Now I don't want to sound
unreasonable but if that boy
keeps on codding round my apple tree
I shall have to give serious thought

to taking my belt to him.

Level II: Don't Rock the Boat

Rung 4: Hardening of Positions

                              I thought
you ought to know that I've let the Crows
walk their Dobermann through my stack of
bean canes behind your chrysanthemum

bed.

Rung 5: Show of Force

            You might like a look at how my
boy John handles his catapult. At
nineteen yards he can hit your green-house
pushing four times out of five.

Rung 6: Significant Mobilisation

                                   I've asked

the wife to call the boy in for his
coffee, get him to look out a good
supply of small stones.

Rung 7: 'Legal' Harassment

                         Sure fire my lawn
spray is soaking your picnic tea-cloth

but I can't be responsible for
how those small drops fall, now can I?

Rung 8: Harassing Acts of Violence

                                   Your

kitten will get a worse clip on her
left ear if she come any nearer

to my rose-bushes, mam.

Rung 9: Dramatic Military Confrontations

Now see here, sonny, I can see you pretty damn clearly up here. If you come one step nearer to that crab-apple tree you'll

get a taste of this strap across your back.

Level III: Nuclear War is Unthinkable

Rung 10: Provocative Diplomatic Break

I'm not going to waste my time gabbing to you any longer, Barnes : I'm taking this telephone off the

hook.

Rung 11: All is Ready Status

Margery, bring that new belt of mine out on the terrace, would you ? I want these crazy coons to see we mean business.

Rung 12: Large Conventional War

Take that, you lousy kraut. My

pop says you're to leave our crab-apple tree alone. Ouch ! Ow ! I'll screw you for that.

Rung 13: Large Compound Escalation

O.K., you've asked for it. The Crows' dog is coming into your lilac

bushes.

Rung 14: Declaration of Limited Conventional War

       Barnes. Can you hear me through this
loud-hailer ? O.K. Well, look. I have
no intention of being the first
to use stones. But I will if you do.

Apart from this I won't let the dog
go beyond your chrysanthemum bed
unless your son actually starts
to climb the tree.

Rung 15: Barely Nuclear War

          Why, no. I never

told the boy to throw a stone. It was
an accident, man.

Rung 16: Nuclear Ultimatum

        Now see here. Why
have you wheeled your baby into the
tool-shed ? We've not thrown stones.

Rung 17: Limited Evacuation

             Honey. I

don't want to worry you but their two
girls have gone round to the Jones's.

Rung 18: Spectacular Show of Force

             John.
Throw a big stone over the tree, would
you : but make sure you throw wide.

Rung 19: Justifiable Attack

            So we

threw a stone at the boy. Because he
put his foot on the tree. I warned you
now, Barnes.

204

Rung 20: Peaceful World-Wide Embargo or Blockade

Listen, Billy, and you too
Marianne, we've got to teach this cod

a lesson. I'm asking your help in
refusing to take their kids in, or
give them any rights of way, or lend
them any missiles until this is

over.

Level IV: No Nuclear Use

Rung 21: Local Nuclear War

John. Give him a small fistful
of bricks. Make sure you hit him, but not
enough to hurt.

Rung 22: Declaration of Limited Nuclear War

Hello there. Barnes. Now
get this, man. I propose to go on

throwing stones as long as your boy is
anywhere near my tree. Now I can
see you may start throwing stones back and
I want you to know that we'll take that

without going for your wife or your
windows unless you go for ours.

Rung 23: Local Nuclear War — Military

We
propose to go on confining our
stone-throwing to your boy beside our

tree : but we're going to let him have
it with all the stones we've got.

Rung 24: Evacuation of Cities — About 70 per cent

Sweetie.
Margery. Would you take Peter and
Berenice round to the Switherings?

Things are getting pretty ugly.

Level V: Central Sanctuary

Rung 25: Demonstration Attack on Zone of Interior

We'll
start on his cabbage-plot with a strike
of bricks and slates. He'll soon see what we
could do if we really let our hands

slip.

Rung 26: Attack on Military Targets

You bastards. Sneak in and smash our
crazy paving, would you?

Rung 27: Exemplary Attacks against Property

We'll go for
their kitchen windows first. Then put a
brace of slates through the skylight.

Rung 28: Attacks on Population

O.K.

Unless they pull out, chuck a stone or
two into the baby's pram in the
shed.

206

Rung 29: Complete Evacuation — 95 per cent

They've cleared the whole family, eh,
baby and all. Just Barnes and the boy

left. Best get your mom to go round to
the Switherings.

Rung 30: Reciprocal Reprisals

Well, if they smash the
bay-window we'll take our spunk out on
the conservatory.

Level VI: Central War

Rung 31: Formal Declaration of General War

Now listen,

Barnes. From now on in we're going all
out against you — windows, flowers, the
lot. There's no hauling-off now without
a formal crawling-down.

Rung 32: Slow-Motion Counter-Force War

We're settling

in for a long strong pull, Johnny. We'd
better try and crack their stone stores one
at a time. Pinch the bricks, plaster the
flowers out and smash every last

particle of glass they've got.

Rung 33: Constrained Reduction

We'll have
to crack that boy's throwing-arm with a
paving-stone. Just the arm, mind. I don't
want him killed or maimed for life.

Rung 34: Constrained Disarming Attack

Right, son.

We'll break the boy's legs with a strike of
bricks. If that fails it may have to come
to his head next.

Rung 35: Counter-Force with Avoidance

There's nothing else for
it. We'll have to start on the other

two up at the Jones's. If the wife
and the baby gets it, too, it can't
be helped.

Level VII: City Targeting

Rung 36: Counter-City War

So it's come to the crunch. His
Maggie against my Margery. The

kids against the kids.

Rung 37: Civilian Devastation

We can't afford
holds barred any more. I'm going all
out with the slates, tools, bricks, the whole damn
shooting-match.

208

Rung 38: Spasm or Insensate War

All right, Barnes. This is it.

Get out the hammer, son : we need our
own walls now. I don't care if the whole
block comes down. I'll get that maniac
if it's the last thing I — Christ. O, Christ.

THE SKI MURDERS

AUTHOR'S NOTE:

Consultants of this encyclopaedia-poem may find it convenient to work according to some arbitrary or appropriate programme dictated by a sequence of letters. These could either be meaningless, e.g., PZTE RFGN QQLX? or (perhaps better) grammatical phrases or sentences, e.g., 'WHO'S FOR TENNIS?' Naturally, one may want to apply the rule of one consultation one letter, so that in the example given the programme will be WHO'S FR TENI? A full reading of the encyclopaedia is not necessary to appreciate the main elements of the story, nor will complete acquaintance with the entries entirely solve the mystery. The ski murders remain the enigma they always were.

Anarak: She felt his warm hand moving against the polished zippers of her pocket. In a moment the cold pouch would be opened, the photographs recovered. Gritting her teeth, she forced her head round and had thrust her shoulder against the laced front of his crimson anarak before the big man could turn. His gloved fist eased back and he grunted as his winded body fell in the hard snow of the toboggan run.

Blood Pressure: It was high, but she would live. Miles knew that. Through the glass wall of her centrally heated bedroom he could see the black flicker of Z-cars (q.v.) in the sound-proofed *après-ski* lounge. Christ, he thought, when *will* they grow up?

Cortina: Inez dipped her cloth in the oil and gently drew it along the curved black blade. There was something sensuous, almost sexual, in this intimate washing and cleaning of such an immaculate and deadly implement. The straps into which her feet went, the long flat under-surface, the uptilted tip — she shivered at the thought of their caress on the crisp snow. Here in Cortina the symbolism of these instruments was appallingly close. She fingered her corduroy vole (q.v.) and lay back on the bloodshot candlewick of the bedspread.

Double Diamond: Cusumba was frightened. The thought of Prestwich's body down there in the sleigh-shed was on his mind. He ordered a second double diamond and watched the dark brown liquid froth from the can with a strange sense of achievement. At least he had not lost the power to order a drink. A Manx band struck up in the patio. He could hear the snow-owls in the pines. Life was a possibility.

Exposure Meter: It seemed to Prestwich as the old Rolleiflex gently bumped the *tête de nègre* behind his fair-isle cardigan that the best hiding place might well be the least expected. He fingered the bakelite exposure meter in its calfskin holder. Here? Not forty yards away the Count was rehearsing his tournament chassis on the packed slopes of the ski-school.

Ferguson: To the Count as he went down for the fourth time on the Chinese pye-dog the pocked leather case on the radiator was a mask of pain. Children's Hour (though how could they pick it up?) came out as a scream. de Montfort was buckling on his puce gauntlets for the *coup de grâce*. There was no time, the Count thought, there was no time. But he rose to his knees and, reaching with bleeding fingers for the tiny black box which could save him, switched the white disc on to Luxembourg. It was accident, but the foreign music stopped the blow.

Genetic Code: With his ice-axe Cusumba hacked the Third U in the wall of the glacier. Overhead he could hear the Sikorski (q.v.) circling. Those great battering wings! Like the yellow hornbills in the elephant's graveyard of the Congo. Would the Irish zeppelin be in time to read the message before the thaw? Already he felt the ice warm to his sweating cheek. He visualised the swollen gold cigar in the clean air of this last resort he had so loved. Raganza came to the mullioned windows of the gondola. He was holding his German binoculars. The black lenses tightened on the distant ice-fall.

Huysmans: Prestwich ran his nail-file across the rough white string of the package. It frayed, broke, curled away on the polished pine-blocks. He began to unwrap the heavy cartridge paper with a sense of mounting excitement. Any moment now he would hold the key to the genetic code (q.v.) in his hands. The book itself, when it fell at last from the underlying tissue, was a disappointment: slim, black, encased in cheap linsen boards. He turned it over in his stubby hands. Could this really be the answer to the problems of Ulster? (q.v.)

Ilinx: The glass bubble spun on its metal wire. As she fought for breath in her gas-mask, Inez could see the world whirling like a storm of snow in a paperweight. Her lashing ski-boot flung open the gilt-edged complete Huysmans (q.v.), and she watched the elaborate pages of *A Rebours* unfurl on the wet rubber as Ellington bent over her prostrate body. In a wave of dizziness she could feel the escalating roundabout of passion engulf her.

Jew's Harp: The Count began to pluck absent-mindedly at the strings of his anarak (q.v.) as he climbed the ski-slope. In the spare pocket of his camera-case there was a small grey musical instrument whose purpose and name he had not yet learnt. His brows furrowed as he strove to remember the definition of a jew's-harp: could that be it? It would all fit — the bedraggled Kafka (q.v.), the doped Weetabix (q.v.), the alert face of Immelman in the helicopter.

Kafka: Ninian accepted the consequences. As she fastened the little capsule against the glue-stiffened entrenchment of the spine, she wondered what Kafka would have thought. That sly, oppressed Czech, that justice-ridden Jew: how could *he* have known the agonies of the secret agent, the midnight hallucinations of the spy in the ski-resort?

Lighter Fuel: The Count squeezed the tiny rubber cylinder in his fingers. The plastic measurer lay glistening slightly in the candle-flame on the edge of his bed. He smelt the exciting, raw odour of petrol. Once, twice, he nipped the pierced end of the little container: and smiled grimly to himself as the bulging drops oozed and dripped into their slowly filling bath. Outside the window, Miles Ellington had moved the catch on his Derringer.

Minox: The matt aluminium felt cool against his burning cheek. He lay in the snow and took it. Give or take five minutes the Italian police would reach the ski station by seven o'clock. Beaumaris had a good start but he could never work the pedals in those clogs. Still, it was a good start. If only the first roll had been developed on Friday! That fourteenth shot of Ninian Rich in the deep end would do the trick. Thank God for the built-in exposure meter (q.v.), Cusumba thought, as he fell back on the vellum Kafka (q.v.).

Nostalgia: The film spread easily over her damp skin. Cool, glossy and crackling, it encased her bosom like a layer of varnish. They would never think to look for it there. For a moment she felt a stab of nostalgia for the old methods, the negatives in the bran barrel, the contact prints listed in a cigar catalogue. But the weakness passed. She was soon striding over the creaking boards of the tea-chalet towards the chair-lift.

Omo: The white suds bubbled in the lavender basin. Inez caught her creamed face in the glass. My God, she thought, what wouldn't I give to be a man for once. Her cool nails moved on the taut skin of her bust, slipped to the side, released the firm catch. In the pale orange light from the wall fitment Ninian watched the proud nipples lift and pout as their pink shell dropped in the foaming bowl. It was several minutes before she grasped the full implications.

Peccary: de Montfort ground his teeth. In the Arnheim zoo once they had fed a peccary together. The fastidious little pig had come on high toes to nibble fudge from her hand. As the wind whipped his bared face in the darkness he began to count the years since anyone had touched his cheek as she had. Pull yourself together, man, he found himself muttering, there is work to be done for the people of Ulster (q.v.).

Quetta: The little bastard just *might* have been born there, too. You never knew. No won-der the English were dying, Inez thought, as she felt once again the magnificent ilinx (q.v.) of the tumbling ski-lift: no wonder, when men like Prestwich were in control. She hugged her mink anarak (q.v.) tighter round her elegant shoulders and watched the sun glinting on the Count's skis.

Rolleiflex: The body of Simon Prestwich lay in the smashed laths of the sleigh-shed. There seemed to be a smell of burnt cordite in the air. Miles knelt beside him, the revolver smoking in his hand. The Rolleiflex they had come to know so well was broken open, the film had gone. Miles buried his head in his hands.

Sikorski: The great fans of the Russian helicopter beat the air. Through the snow-encrusted perspex Immelman could see the tiny black figure far below on the glacier. What was the stupid bastard doing there? He slipped the brown octagon of a zube between his teeth and crunched thoughtfully as his wasp-coloured machine hovered over the snow-fields. There was work to do here for the de-coding unit at a quick guess.

Tête de Nègre: Miles Ellington allowed the blade to sink at its own speed through the choco-late-studded ball on his plate.

213

Very few of these were available at such lofty altitudes, he knew, and of those no more than a quarter were impregnated to the full with the real Spanish sherry he could so surely taste the flavour of in this one. He paused with the last morsel half way to his lips as the sound of a muffled explosion came to his ears. It had come from somewhere down there in the fir plantation.

Ulster: What on earth were they doing it for, de Montfort asked himself in the freezing men's-room. For a one-horse republic in an under-populated island? Not even for that: for a two-bit dependency of the English Empire. As he drew the silver teeth together in his groin, a hair caught and he cursed, fluently, in Yiddish. Outside, the Irish lace of the snow fell like a judgment on the half-buried pages of *The Castle*.

Vole: Inez Lawson-Emery had nothing on. Not even the radio, Cusumba reflected, as he pressed his bloodshot eye against the ivory key escutcheon of her bedroom door. In the nun-shaped aperture of cream and gold fur exposed to the eye the most striking novelty was the maroon corduroy vole on her dressing-table. Its beady eye stared fixedly into his own beside the superb coppery but-tocks enthroned on their Danish leather stool. Now, he thought, and was through the door with his hand on the shutter as the long tanned body rose to its full height on the pony-skin.

Weetabix: Of course, there would really have been eighteen to the packet: but Miles Elling-ton had other things to think about as he pasted down the cardboard flap of his elaborate decoy. Licking salt from his fingers he tipped the last spoon-ful of strawberry Yoghurt down his throat and rose to leave the table. That porrage-hating nig-ger was in for a thin time with his orange juice.

Xenia: Yes, it was there, once; at Nauplion, in winter. Nobody left but the regulars and Miles. I saw him first in the sun-lounge with his feet on a Moorish coffee-table, reading Huysmans (q.v.). We exchanged the usual greetings. I in my squalid pull-over, he in his Chester-Barry two-piece. Over an ouzo we hatched The Plan.

Yoghurt: The little jar rested lightly in Ellington's bronzed fingers. Nothing disturbed the early evening silence but the click of spoons. He licked his lips. That stupid breakfast food would have to do the job. Cor-tina was hardly the place for gun-play. And that little affair of the Count's broken rib-cage had taken some hushing up. If only the old yobbo had learned to ski. With a single smooth movement the spy rose and turned as Cusumba's grin blockaded the doorway.

Z-Cars: Ninian slid her long legs one by one into the tight elastic sheath of her midnight blue stretch pants. There would scarcely be room for an extra fountain pen in these, she reflected, as she studied the silent unrolling of Z-cars on the foreign screen. What use would sound have been in a language of which she knew no single word save the one for making love?

FIN DU GLOBE

RULES:

The game is best played with a dealer and four players who are known as North, South, East and West. The pack consists of 52 postcards and 4 *fin du globe* cards which should be shuffled by the dealer before each reading. An approximately equal number of cards should be handed by the dealer to each of the four players. These cards may be arranged in any order provided they are kept face down until they are read. Players must read the first card in their hand when called on by the dealer who may call them in any order he chooses provided the same player is not called on twice running. Each hand is terminated by the first player who turns up and reads out one of the four *fin du globe* cards. The game is best played in three hands.

Seatoller: *The Captain to Rodrigo*

It has rained every day. Indeed, the annual mean rainfall here is the highest in England. We can only get the photographs by bubble-car. I can hardly believe that Millicent is lonely, but keep the dogs leashed. I shall write later.

Bogota: *Courtelle to Sigmund*

In the hills they say there are Indians who believe in the myth of the Flood. We shall need their resolution. My love to Johnny. But don't do anything yet about the van Loon. The tide may turn.

Karachi: *Sigmund to the Captain*

I am feeling a little sick. Last night I discovered a copy of your book with a bullet-hole in the spine. The heat is certainly terrific. If the Chinese attack again, there is nothing for it but to cede the Nagas. Without machine-guns we are nothing.

Inishboffin: *Raymond Allister to Elvira Norman*

There is no hope. Verne is aware of the stresses, but what can he do? If only we had artillery! The North Col is a possible route, as you say. But I think the Bishop should go in first.

Andritsaina:
Nicholas Emery to Commander Singal

I have just picked up the news from the South Gap on the Gabo transistor. We must act soon in the Cheddar Gorge. Despite the weather the temple was looking extremely sexy. I signed my name in the visitor's book in a thunderstorm. Klebben is drying out by the fire.

Algiers:
Philippa to Mrs Noakes

This morning I found a scarab inside a packet of crystallised figs. Of course, it may all be coincidence. We asked the porter, but he speaks no German. I am resting behind the fourth window from the left on the third floor of the small chateau in the foreground. Remember there are only four more days.

Samarcand:
Rivers to Favorita

The airship is well on its way to Afghanistan. In this climate the Captain should be over the Gulf by Sunday. The Casbah is alive with rumours. Why don't the Hussars advance in the Khyber? How far is Alaric from Moscow?

Tristan da Cunha:
Sybil to Runciman

The midget submarines are already off Corsica. The Bishop will send you full instructions by the helicopter. If Bridget won't believe you, wire for a new propeller. And keep the lines clear. The ball is at everyone's feet now.

Neueschwanstein:
Sir Roger Green to Rodrigo

I arrived yesterday. The soap is atrocious. From my bedroom window I can see the bridge which Wagner mentions in Parsifal. How Eric kept the Exchequer intact is a mystery. Remember that if all else fails we may still be able to enter Liechtenstein by the cable-car.

Fort Worth:
The Bishop to Amos Long

I have had to work my electric razor from the light socket. The *son et lumière* is magnificent but the rockets have kept me awake half the night. Watch out for the movements of the Baltic Squadron. I anticipate a disastrous fall in Consols. My blessing to Peter and Paul.

Mexico City: *Miss Emily Nonesince to Commander Singal*

The new stamps are extremely indecent. They show the *voladores* with nothing on but wings. I know the camera works, but we cannot afford to take any risks. I shall try to get a message through by the Thunderbird. We must be patient, liebchen.

Montevideo: *Ludovic Meyer Smith to Miss Emily Nonesince*

I apologise for the cigarette burn. This morning our embassy was incinerated by the Czech insurgents. Mountjoy has taken refuge in the docks. We shall try to ship him out in an orange-box. I recommend a red alert for the passenger pigeons.

Ballyshannon: *The Bishop to Earl Boyes*

The Portuguese destroyers have relieved Marangatam. Sir Giles was caught — quite literally — with his trousers down. The Exchange is cock-a-hoop. I have put my shirt on gilt-edged. What a lovely thing the Bloody Foreland is!

Melbourne: *Perrutz and Nellie to Sir Roger Green*

Mandryk is inconsolable. An anarchist has poisoned one of these bears with a eucalyptus leaf. How is Natchka? The Sydney papers are full of the gliding trials on Helvellyn. I think the imperial fleet will move in the Baltic.

Ottawa: *Sir Lucas Crowther to Otto van Fleet*

Do you know that when the French advanced they picked out Jeremy by his green cockade? I believe the Orange-men are still at bay in the Maddermarket. Why ever did Nancy paint them in slick greys? Fenris has learnt to bark in Morse. But the sky is black with Finnish caravelles.

Salt Lake City: *Rodrigo to Courtelle*

This morning Boris was killed by an air-gun pellet outside the Tabernacle. The police have made extensive enquiries but no-one can shed any light on either the motive or the possible culprit. As you see, it is a long building a little like a sugar loaf. I have suffered a mild recurrence of orchitis. Perhaps I shall buy a chihuahua.

218

Amalfi:
*Sprock to
The Captain*

In the Cloister of Paradise this morning I encountered a small boy with a wen. He is not, of course, in the picture. Gretchen has bought a bikini embroidered with turtles in white silk. For breakfast yesterday we ate a new species of cray-fish. Alaric is well.

Mykonos:
*Lord Maundy to
Miss Anstruther*

We are surely safe here, not three miles from Apollo's lions. I have hired myself a flat in the village. It is all yellow now, from the rays. If the Captain rings tonight, I am ready. Believe me, Gwendoline, we are going under with all flags flying.

Pitcairn Island:
*Commander Singal
to Squadron Leader
Baring*

We boarded the S.S. Paradise off Tongareva. The crew put up a stiff fight, but we cracked the hold. There were forty-three Malayan rifles in banana-cases. Now do you see we must intervene in Penang? I am writing this full steam ahead for Guayaquil.

Entebbe: *Solly Jaggers
to the
Queen of Windhoek*

The Albertville Regatta was a great success. Our probation officers were the pride of Mozambique in their coonskin loincloths. This turbulence in the zinc mines must soon subside. Majesty, we are both in up to our necks. But wait and see, we shall laugh together in Broken Hill.

Basalt Springs: *Adolphus
Pratt to
Squadron Leader Baring*

We are eight thousand feet above. Copenhagen. Observe the clarity of the air. I have ridden all morning in a Western saddle. At night our satellites are like gems in the Queen of Sheba's diadem. I know we shall win.

Rotterdam: *Miss
Anstruther to Courtelle*

The marijuana was in the joystick. You had better make your getaway in the Puss Moth. I suggest a straight course over Chesham and Princes Risborough. Remember what Jacob said. There is no meaning or purpose; only the codes.

219

Lyme Regis:

Morgan
Everest to
Sir Linstock Esher

They will get me in five minutes. I have four slugs left. Here in the Shell Tower, my leader, the last outpost of Western values is crumbling. What wouldn't I give for a thimbleful of taquila! Christ, they are coming.

King George V Land:

Felix
Emberton to
Miss Alison Peery

I have bound your *Meditations* in seal-skin. The hovercraft is an asset, but what shall we do for bear-spears? The prefabricated igloos were not a success. The last John Collinson is alive with woodmites. Dear Alison, I am snow-blind, I cannot see the Winkles.

Astrakhan:

The Bishop
to Lynx Raffles

Canadian Javelins have dropped four points. I am transferring a million rupees to Hercules Powder. The MSS are safe in Foochow. Who knows which way the mandarins will jump? I played a hand of mah jong with Clovis yesterday.

Havana:

Sir Linstock Esher
to Alvarez da Sala

War has broken out with Albania. The Guatemalan auxiliaries have embarked in the Q-boat. I see no hope of a victory at Rifa Chiffa. Here on the quay the Chinese laundrymen are in arms for new mangles. A reward is out for Angus McFlyte.

Porsanger Fjord:

Alvarez da
Sala to
Ensign Lascelles

Our ambassador has handed an ultimatum to the Gambian Foreign Minister. There is no hope of a settlement with the Greeks. If the English back their minelayers in the Skagerrak, we are done for. I am playing gin rummy with a Lapp chiropodist. Grizelda has had poor hands.

Vaduz:

Courtelle to Rivers

Our armed forces have multiplied eight times. Here they are in their goatskin tunics. Given but resolution, we could hold the pass for thirteen days with pea-shooters. What news, by the way, of Lynx Raffles? The Prince relies on his total annihilation of the Kurds at Orenburg.

Wanganui:

Clovis to Alaric

The boys have taken the whole thing very well. We all went into the shelters singing the *Te Deum*. Runciman smashed the R.G.2 but we got the second stanza on the ribbon mike. I am very puzzled about the news from the Swiss border. How ever does Atalanta hope to win?

Groningen:

Earl Boyes to Sister Eakins

It is sealing wax, not blood, my darling. I have had to melt it over a paraffin lamp in the larder. Whiskers shall have a tin of ginger biscuits, but not for another day. Tonight I can think of nothing except our defeat in the Estuary of the Plate. They say the Amazons were superb.

Pretoria:

Lynx Raffles to Morgan Everest

The Glue Factory is already under pressure. These damned Watutsi take some grinding-down. The over-print is a joke, of course, but they do need volunteers. I am dead beat. They taught me the word for jig-a-jig in Swahili.

Curaçao:

The Queen of Windhoek to The Captain

The artificial whale is already inside the harbour. Momssen has cabled that every man will do his duty. Five, four, three, two, one, zero. That was it. Congratulate me, Solly, the whole of Bolivia is in Javan hands.

Starbuck Island:

The Queen of Windhoek to The Captain

The P.G.N. commando has landed at West Point. Sir Hilary has held the four beaches, but Nathan says it is only time. I remember once at Cape Farewell we beat them back with soup-ladles. Here by the swamp I can smell the peccaries. I am not enamoured of a life of whale-steaks.

Sevastopol:

The Captain to Favorita

I believe Mountjoy was shot with a German-ground Beretta. The ace of spades was found tucked in his left trouser turn-up. I have had to live on caviare. And this view of the Black Sea is not original. Still, we persist.

221

Grootfontein:

Elvira
Norman to
Simon Hardcastle

I have caught and tamed a whistling hyena. Alas, his dung is the colour of grapefruit juice. First it was fluoride and now these pills. I would willingly drown the Queen of Windhoek in her African cointreau. Have these people no shame?

Dar Es Salaam:

Tregenza
to Sigmund

You remember what Nietschze said about the tortoise? This is it. I have never eaten so many betel-nuts in my life. The jeeps are still hunting for Peregrine in the Bong. The rhinoceros detail has withdrawn, of course, but the compensation is still a very open question.

Amritsar:

Strangeways
to Manley

There are strikes in the manganese refinery. The polo ponies are dying of rickets at Simla. They tell me that Crazy Horse has escaped from Berlinnie. With that hair-do he can hardly hire a jaguar. Still, it is no smiling matter.

San Marino:

Canon
Slocombe to
Amos Long

The zeppelins were a fine sight from the rampart. How I wonder what Raymond Allister would have thought! We played a few hands of *bézique* once in the *pensione*. He was always a lover of good cigars. Remember to send my driving licence.

Easter Island:

Sangster
and Forbes to
Canon Slocombe

We saw the bombers go overhead this morning. It seemed as if all the gods were craning their necks to look. I have finished the second volume of your Treitschke. There is no more moving analysis in the language. We are spending most of our time in the sea.

Novosibirsk:

Runciman to
Ludovic Meyer Smith

We are out of shillings for the gas-meter. I am writing this in my balaclava. Even the opera has closed. I shall try to break the road-blocks with a snowplough. But I think we are trapped.

Angmagsalik: *Nicholas Emery to Professor Stolz*

The last Arabian was four feet tall. We found his body three hundred yards from the filling-station. There were skeletons of a hundred mice in the spars of a bran-tub. They must have had it rough. Remember me to Mrs Noakes.

Beersheba: *Julius Andover to Simon Hardcastle*

I deeply regret the news from Helsingfors. If the barricades are up in the flea-market, let Felix Emberton retire. I know my longhand is appalling, but persevere, Simon. I am bleeding from the groin. And they shot my secretary.

Peking: *Ensign Lascelles to the Burgomaster of Coventry*

I have burned a hole in my sou'wester with the electric iron. The perils of travelling! I have just heard the news. The giant pandas have stripped the bamboo forests as far as Kanchenjunga. What on earth can have caused this population explosion?

Mauritius: *Sir Lucas Crowther to The Captain*

I am sheltering in the smallest room of the Lithuanian consulate. Forgive my handwriting. The illuminations are distracting. Jellaby did all he could, but the zebra-men were too much. In five minutes I shall make a dash for the mail-van.

Taormina: *Amos Long to Patch Codron*

I can hear the Greek maids hoovering the Captain's bedroom. I hope the bloodstains will respond to the spot-lifter. It was quite a party. We got the first four with the Maxim gun, but Repetto escaped in the bread-lift. To think that Garibaldi set out from such a tiny bay!

South Shields: *McFlayle to Mr Evans*

I am on my way to the Richmond Trailer Festival. There are broken Rileys in all the lay-bys. For an hour and half we shall pay our homage to Wisley and Deans. If only Algy would use the apple and biscuit mine. We could break the Tay Boom with a single charge.

223

Paranagua:

Favorita to
Lord Maundy

I have won four thousand milreis at the animal game. Alicia had bought a handbag of ostrich-skin, so I played the crocodile. One should never jump to conclusions. They say da Sala has broken all records at the Durban Book Fair. My respects to the Duke of Tandy.

Aberdeen:

Repetto to
Sprock

The herring-boats are full of poisoned mackerel. The dead lobster is in the creel. I am typing this to be shown at once to Elvira Norman. Tell your beads, my dear, for a sick retriever. And keep your fingers crossed.

Conway Castle:

Lieutenant Flyte to
Commander Singal

We are down to the last barrel of apples. Bartholomew has fled. The men are living on dead mice. I have tested the life-belts, but even the rubber has perished. I am emptied of everything except the desire to hold out for another day.

Kanazawa:

Mrs Noakes
to the
Duke of Tandy

Away we go on my new Corona Marauder! And what a victory for our men in the Hinge of Borneo! The Creole paratroops are already shelling the Community Centre. Here on the sixth floor I can hear the volcano. I must try sleeping with ear-plugs.

Castelvetrano:

Millicent
to Sir Lucas Crowther

I am reading the sonnets of Gertrude Thimbleby. There is nothing like them in English. Father, I know, you are off to Mangalore. Let Amber advance one single reason why this koati should die. I am ill with hate.

Palermo:

Sigmund to
Perrutz and Nellie

This morning my hearing-aid was broken at Monreale. I can hardly believe it was an accident. In the Corpus Christi procession Vencini spat in the gutter as he passed below their posters. Here at the *Britannique* the sea-food is excellent. But how can it last?

LADY DRACULA

Lady Dracula
Flies into my mind,
I hear her wings whistle
An' her teeth grind.

Lady Dracula
With long black hair,
Lady Dracula
With red fangs bare

Lady Dracula
Is hungry for blood,
She digs deep in
An' she sucks real good.

Lady Dracula
With long black hair,
Lady Dracula
With red fangs bare

Lady Dracula
Was once alive,
She drinks men's blood
From nine till five.

Lady Dracula
With long black hair,
Lady Dracula
With red fangs bare

When the sun rises,
She goes to bed,
Lady Dracula :
You'll find her dead.

Lady Dracula
With long black hair,
Lady Dracula
With red fangs bare

THE SEVEN ROOMS

I

In the first room
a crone
in leather boots
has a hole gashed
in her belly.

An ape in armour
strokes her hips.

I touch you, very gently

II

In the second room
a pair of buttocks
piss
through a barred window
into a funnel
on the back of a cask.

A man drinks it.

I touch you, very gently

III

In the third room
a helmet
with its mouth open
goads a fish
in boots
to swallow a rat.

I touch you, very gently

229

IV

In the fourth room
a nun
with webbed feet
fries a face
in a pan.

I touch you, very gently

V

In the fifth room
a pig
with an oven for a stomach
squats
under a toad.

I touch you, very gently

VI

In the sixth room
a platypus
carries a naked man
on a spit.

A cowled head
walks behind.

I touch you, very gently

VII

In the seventh room
a lizard
drives a blade
through its own throat.

They call this *The Last Judgement.*

I touch you, very gently

EPISODE FROM A FORTNIGHT IN HELL

On the thirteenth day
a tiny silver snail
with a sword through its neck
screams on a rock.

Armies quiver and lunge
like porcupines.

Dinosaurs, or perhaps
camels,
mount a hill towards a castle.

On a stone
like a toad, corpses
are grouped,
ready for shovelling into the ravine.

They call this *Understanding Each Other's Point of View.*

THE MAYERLING DREAM

At dead of night
In pouring rain
I dress your body
Inside my brain.

> *Mary Vetsera*
> *Died at Mayerling*
> *Rudolf shot her*
> *Through the head*
>
> *I am dead, and you are dead*

At mid morning
In fallen snow
The wheels turn
And we travel slow.
It all happened
Long ago.

> *Mary Vetsera*
> *Died at Mayerling*
> *Rudolf shot her*
> *Through the head*
>
> *I am dead, and you are dead*

The bed stood
Where the altar stands.
Baron Stockau
Crossed her hands.

In a black coach
Upon my knees
I ride with your body
Through bare trees.

H*   233

Mary Vetsera's
Ring is gold,
Her hair is white
And her hands are cold.

The wheels turn
And the roads wind,
It all happened
In my mind.

Mary Vetsera
Died at Mayerling,
Rudolf shot her
Through the head

I am dead, and you are dead

STRASSENBAHN

Gut-squeal.

I hear it all night in my dream.

Between rails
and wire,
it worries through the Ring-circuit
like a rat in a maze.

No wonder it squeals.

Gas-worm.

Eating its way out of a street of graves.

DIE NAMENLOSEN

One with a bugle,
slash of gold,
over his shoulder.

The rest, grey gums.

They gnash forward,
swine's-flesh,
into rancid meat.

Only, this was the first war.

They oar in slime,
as out of Auschwitz.

CRANACH'S HUNTS

I

On the first afternoon
they go out of the white city
into the wood.

One with a flat
red hat
has a feathered neck
on his lance.

One with a black hat
is upon a doe
with his sheathed sword.

In the folded
grey sheets of the river
the stags are dying.

Branched heads
waver like water-weeds.

On the bank
seven dogs
beset a hooped one.

Thrown as if
by a tree
one lies in a mat
of its own blood.

In a nearby boat
ladies in long dresses
are rowing.

237

One is being
groped
by a friar.

The spire of
the church
and the blue peak
assure the world
of a fine day.

After all, the king is hunting.

II

On the second afternoon
they have crossed the
bridge
and are in the firs

with their white swords
erect.

Head down
a stag
is already
under their hooves.

The tongues
of the dogs
flicker
over its body.

In threshed
water
the rest
move their
crowns of thorns.

Today
the ladies
make the shapes of breasts
with their bows.

The church
is nowhere to be seen.

Far off,
the city is roofed in blood.

In a green clearing
all the does in the world
walk naked
before a serving-man
in a grey helmet.

The light
still glistens in their pupils.

The date is 1544.

It might have been yesterday.

THE AUSCHWITZ RAG

It's a gas,
            going to the gas,
            going to the gas,
it's a gas, Man,
            going to the gas

I walk on tip-toe
To the Zyklon B,
They're goin' to crucify
Little me.

Up ahead
Stick men in boots,
Crosses over their
Hatchet suits.

The colonel gestures
When I strip.
I spit at him
An' he feels real hip.

Rip them knickers
Off and dance,
I hear you
Can really prance.

Down go my briefs
An' I step out bare,
I show my pussy
Like at a fair.

I make that colonel
Stiff as a post,
With his mouth open
Like he seen a ghost.

Jesus-naked
There in the snow,
I see the crema-
torium glow.

Writhe, body,
Against his fly,
I'm gonna kill you
Before I die.

Jerk off, Man,
For the Fatherland,
I'm juicin' your gun
With my other hand.

Some die by gas,
Some die by knives,
I've used up all
Of my nine lives.

Cool cat, cool cat,
I hear you scream.
Here endeth
The Auschwitz dream.

It's a gas,
going to the gas,
going to the gas,
it's a gas, Man,
going to the gas

SCENES FROM A HISTORY BOOK

I

A short man
with a pinched look
and a high moustache
walks fast
up the Judengasse.

They try to sell him
a leather jacket,
a black Homburg hat,
a pair of driving-gloves.

He shakes his head,
thrusting his hands
in the pockets of his
belted raincoat.

There is a cold wind.

They laugh,
exchange words
in their fur-lined overcoats.

He hurries on
to the Rathausplatz.

There is a lot to do.

No, he is not Napoleon.
It is 1913.
I give you three guesses who he is.

II

Where did they come from?

They came from
a village in Poland.

These are the cheap tailors
who died in Warsaw.

There are shreds of hair
still on their shoulders,
gold teeth in their pockets.

We never knew, we never knew

It is 1945.

They walk towards
a concrete room
in another city.

I hear the shot.

They laugh,
warming their hands
at the body burning.

Any old hair, any old gold

I smell the petrol
burning flesh
flames rising
black smoke
old clothes
old clothes

Who'll give a penny for Hitler's clothes?

WRITTEN ON THE ROAD OF CEMETERIES LEADING TO THE AIRPORT AT VIENNA

I see American poetry
with red claws
conquering the world.

It makes a Vietnam
in the Pushkin industry.

It calls the sonnet
Robert Bly.

Somewhere under the fingers of
Galway Kinnell
James Wright
Anne Sexton
an old man
rusts
in a bottle.

The revolution
starts in his breathing :

One two, one two

Forgotten balloons
are inflated
with names like pantoum.

A hundred poets
rise as one
towards the black mountains.

Bombs are in
their hands,
elegant pieces of sugar
from Little Rock.

244

They drive American poetry
back to the wigwams
where an old Indian
rusts
in an elk-horn.

The revolution
starts in his breathing :

one two, one two

I see European poetry
with red claws
conquering the world.

It makes a Vietnam
in the Whitman industry.

It calls free verse
Adrian Henri.

Write the rest for yourself.

THE PAINTER'S MODEL

I was born in Rome from the yolk of eggs
With a bit of mosaic between my legs.

In Byzantium, I was plated and screwed
Until they discovered *The Art of The Nude.*

Van Eyck was an early performer in flesh,
He laid me under a fine gold mesh.

Hieronymus Bosch had a fertile mind,
He blew me with a clarinet, from behind.

Leonardo was a sadistic bleeder,
I couldn't stand swans, so he made me Leda.

Brueghel was a vicious Flemish brute,
I was varnished by him in my birthday suit.

With Lucas Cranach, life was grim,
There were gropes in water, and then a hymn.

Tintoretto took me along a tunnel,
And a brace of disciples felt up my funnel.

Canaletto made me the colour of rum,
When he oiled my vagina it made me come.

Vermeer of Delft was the first voyeur,
I stripped for his mirror, to make quite sure.

With Rubens, it was the Sabine Rapes
On an apparatus like a bunch of grapes.

Anthony Van Dyke gave me V.D.
On the back of a sinewy horse, with a flea.

As for Boucher, that versatile frog,
He enjoyed me backwards across a log.

David, the bastard, gave me a dose,
And besides that, he was one of those.

Ingres, too, was inclined to be queer,
He tickled my nipples with a Roman spear.

With Delacroix it was chain-mail vests
And discharging his musket across my breasts.

In England, Rossetti soaped my belly
With what he called pre-Raphaelite jelly.

Burne-Jones needed the boots and hair,
His palette seemed blunted when I was bare.

With Auguste Renoir, I shared a punt,
Only things went blurred when he kissed my —

With Picasso I nearly did my nut,
I was taken to bits by him, in a hut.

As for Braque, with his *nature morte*,
I don't find all that corpse stuff sport.

With Salvador Dali, life was worse,
He had beetles crawling when I got the curse.

I died at last, a kinetic Venus,
And Jim Dine embalmed me in a polythene penis.

DOCTOR CRIPPEN'S ELIMINATION KIT

I

I had to get twenty-six
To qualify
So I started with Alvarez.
After all, who needs it,
I always say.
He got leukaemia.

II

The B choice
Was easy.
Sir John had just been inspecting
A Victorian wharf.
I pushed him off it.
The bubbles were worthy of Millais.

III

For Kevin
I made it 1940.
Squadron-Leader Crossley-Holland
DSO, DFC (and bar)
Got his near Biggin Hill.
Causley is editing the letters.

IV

The Poet-Laureate
Was an obvious choice.
I hung about outside the Albert Hall
While Cecil finished his *Elegies*.
Then I let the bomb off
Under the balcony.

V

I couldn't be too choosy
Amidst the Es.
I let Empson have it
With a Chinese throwing-knife.
You must be joking, he said.
He died laughing.

VI

Roy Fuller
Was so much in Oxford
I had to rush about a lot.
I grew a bit tired of Magdalen Barge
Before he swallowed
The poison crumpet.

VII

What with Gunn in America
And Graves in Majorca
The double bill was difficult.
I got the pair of them over
To a conference on syllabics.
They died of boredom.

VIII

When Ted Hughes
Heard I was coming,
He hid under a dahlia.
I mistook him for a field-mouse
And that was that.
Never be a nature poet.

IX

As for Zofia Ilinska,
She died wondering
When someone was going to remember her.
Useful to be an eye
Overlooking all those Japanese fishermen
And do it well.

X

Elizabeth Jennings
Kept things lady-like.
It meant another trip to Oxford
But, after all,
One can't knife everyone
With their own knitting.

XI

James Kirkup
Had to come back from Japan
Specially.
When I rouged his nipples
And hung him over a bath of acid,
Nobody fainted.

XII

Philip Larkin
Met Christopher Logue
On a bridge in Hull.
They fought well for two minutes
Then dived hand in hand
To the jaws of the reviewers.

XIII

Hugh Macdiarmid
Was heard saying
I hear there's a king of Scotland
Who didna write in Lallans,
The Sassenach bastard !
Thus choking.

XIV

Well, when Adrian Mitchell
And Roger McGough
Had finished looking modest
About why *they* weren't in there,
I threw Norman Nicholson
Down a mine-shaft.

XV

Philip Oakes
Appeared on Television
Eulogising the Movement.
Unfortunately, his bowels moved,
No doubt with compassion,
At just the wrong moment.

XVI

Brian Patten
Was caught admiring his profile.
The glass broke
And cut him up.
Liverpool school-girls
Are still living off the pieces.

XVII

As there was no-one
Queueing,
I had to incarcerate William Plomer
In that cupboard with his thigh,
And hang Peter Porter
For horse-stealing.

XVIII

As for Peter Redgrove,
That was the Cornish sickness.
A familiar spirit
Fixed him with a basilisk eye
And carried him off to Cambridge,
Squeaking.

XIX

Stephen Spender, alas,
Ate a marshmallow
With a ball-bearing inside it.
The C.I.A. are still trying
To ferret out
Who put it there.

XX

R. S. Thomas
Tried the Welsh marches once too often.
That flinty face
Walked into a chalk wall
And never came out.
So perish all priestly poets.

XXI

Absence of Us
Left space for a few more Ts,
Like Anthony Thwaite.
I fancy a Roman coin
Dropped in his gizzard
At the age of a hundred and eighty.

XXII

For the same reason
Tarn and Tomlinson
Met Tonks and Tiller
At a wake for absent Vs.
Quadruple disintegration :
All four got on each other's wicks.

XXIII

Laurence Whistler
Engraved his own fate in glass.
Unfortunately,
Someone shattered it
Shouting messages
At a deaf man, possibly David Wright.

XXIV

So John Wain,
Big John,
Enjoyed the place marked with an x.
On Treasure Island
Long John Silver
Greased his palm with dollars.

XXV

Andrew Young
Died of immortality.
At his age
What more do you do
Except live on
Burrowed in years, like a mole ?

XXVI

At the end
When it was Z-time,
I took the waters myself.
Beckoning to the waitress,
Without more ado,
I stepped ashore onto the scaffold.